A GUIDE TO OVER 1000
OF THE BEST
EVANGELICAL BOOKS IN PRINT

KREGEL USED BOOKS
PO BOX 2607
GRAND RAPIDS MI 49501
PHONE: (616) 459-9444
TOLL FREE FAX: 888-USD-BOOK
E-MAIL: USEDBOOKS@KREGEL.COM
WEB: WWW.KREGEL.COM

BASIC BOOKS FOR THE MINISTER'S LIBRARY

By
DAVID W. BROOKMAN, M.A.
Harrisonburg, Virginia
1986

Published by:
Destiny Image Publishers
P. O. Box 351
Shippensburg, PA 17257   717-532-3040
For Worldwide Distribution

Affectionately dedicated
to
LINDA
my devoted and beloved
wife

Contents

Foreword

David W. Brookman, M.A., and I have been close friends and colleagues in the ministry for many years. It was in Bible college that we first met. It became very plain to me that David had a love for books and was always anxiously making brief notes regarding the author and contents of these books. This soon became a continued policy that he followed and later published a book on *Recommended Reading Books,* which proved to be very valuable in many cases.

I was reminded the other day of how Paul told Timothy "to study to show thyself approved unto God, a workman that needeth not to be ashamed, rightly dividing the Word of truth." (II Timothy 2:15). This has become a very important message to all who will handle the Word of God inasmuch as improper handling of the Word of God may result in eternal death and damnation of precious souls for whom Christ died. One is able to make corrections in other fields of labor, but when handling the eternal truth, one must be careful of their proclamation to make sure they are correct.

The author, having been well acquainted with books for many years and in devoting much of his time in the investigation of these books, has listed in his book entitled, *Basic Books for the Minister's Library,* over a thousand of the very best evangelical books in print today. The thing one will appreciate so much about the author is that he has not listed just the books that cannot be purchased or books that are long out of print, but ones that are in print and may be obtained and added to one's library today. Every minister, Bible college professor, pastor, evangelist, and student will find this commentary to be a tremendous blessing to them and to their work. In a day when individuals are concerned about the conservation of time and making good use of their time, they need books to assist them and books for their library that will help them.

It is amazing how this author has used his skills and love for books, together with being cognizant of the ministerial needs at all levels of ministry, in the compilation of this excellent volume. This book is divided into ten sections and a short introduction to the subject opens each section. Then each book is annotated indicating its contents, audience, (that is, beginner or advanced readers) and the theological viewpoint. I am convinced that every one will find this book to be a must for them regardless of the level of ministry they are on, and will be able to utilize it to assist them in the procuring of books needed for their library and ministry.

Inasmuch as the author has spent many hours compiling his writings and information, and it is so easily obtainable, I am certain that each individual will find this book to be a tremendous blessing. I count it a high honor to be able to write the foreword for such an excellent volume and commend it to each one.

Howard V. Spruill, D. Min.
District Superintendent
Potomac District Council

Introduction

Today's minister finds himself beset by pressures which make his purchases of books a task he should handle with care. One of these pressures is the economic squeeze that reaches from the supermarket to the bookstore. The second problem is that so many books are coming from the religious presses that minister's need counsel regarding the value and content of each. In addition to these, the pastor's time limitations place a pressure upon him to exercise seriousness as he seeks those volumes which yield the best results to his total ministry.

In spite of all such pressures the minister of today needs good, workable tools to fulfill his Biblical responsibilities. So it becomes needful to have a book to assist the minister in his choice of the best religious books in print today. Such a book would also put a rein on the book-buying impulsiveness of many ministers! This book shall attempt to give guidance in the choice and use of religous books for every minister. Unlike the book that I wrote about the minister's library in 1971, I will only list books that are in print as of 1986. Please be advised that the best books are not always the latest books. In fact, it is this authors opinion, that some of the best books are the older ones. Fortunately, most of the best older works are now in print.

This book has been prepared for ministers of all age-levels who deal with books in performing the various tasks of the Christian ministry. The aim is simple: to aid in finding a profitable path through the endlessly growing jungle of religious books. It should be noted that this book is not written for the scholar or professor. It is to be basic and practical. This is not to say that the scholar or professor may not profit from its use, but its primary aim is to those preparing for the ministry or to those already functioning in the Christian ministry.

The book has been written within the framework of the historical evangelical Protestant tradition rooted in wholehearted obedience to the authority of Scriptures. This does not mean, however, that all the books discussed are absolutely "safe" or "sound." Their inclusion is not intended to lead some astray but to make their reading experience flexible and well-rounded. Keeping these things in mind, I have listed the most significant works of individuals irrespective of their denominational affiliation. This means that I will be recommending some of the best books on the market today from several theological slants.

This book is divided into ten sections. A short introduction to the subject opens each section. Each book is then annotated indicating its content, audience (beginners or advanced readers), and theological viewpoint. I will not attempt to list all of these for each book. Clearly there is no need to be exhaustive; rather the emphasis is on selectivity with brief annotations.

A study library is a personal thing. Just as different people have different tastes and interests in life, so too will a minister's library reflect his interests, tastes, and needs as an individual and a Christian worker. How well your library fits your personal needs will determine much of your success as a minister. Great care should be exercised in determining your exact needs and then tailoring your library to fill those needs.

Years ago Bacon said, "Reading maketh a full man." A universal mark of a called minister of the Gospel is an insatiable thirst for Bible knowledge, and reading is one sure path to intellectual growth. To those of his people who had no taste for reading, John Wesley said commandingly that they must acquire it! Alexander Whyte, advised, "Sell your shirt and buy books." Even the Apostle Paul the author of the most profound treatises the Church will ever know, after all those wonderful years of evangelism, in the last days of his life on earth, knowing that at any time he might be called out of the Mamertime Prison to lay down his life for Christ, asked Timothy to bring "the books and the parchments." He never lost his love for reading.

Finally, I wish to thank Dr. Howard V. Spruill, for his encouragement to write this book and for so graciously writing the foreword. I want to thank my fellow ministers and Bible college and seminary students, for their encouragement to write this book. I am also indebted to my Bible college and Seminary professors that shared their expertise with me over the past several years in the area of books. Many years and hours of laborious research have gone into its making. The book has grown out of my experience as a pastor, as a Bible college and Seminary guest lecturer, and as an adjunct professor of homiletics at a Seminary. My thanks to all.

General Reference Books on the Bible

The wise minister will gather about him only quality reference books. But the supreme reference book is the Bible itself. The Bible is God's revelation of what He is like and what He requires us to do. Since the Bible comes from the ancient world, it needs to be explained because it was written in other languages by men of other cultures. God chose to reveal Himself through the Hebrew, Aramaic and Greek languages at certain definite times in specific cultures. How can one get information about the Bible in its original form and time? Through the means of the Bible itself and good reference books.

It is not enough to learn about what meaning the Bible had for people in Bible times, we must learn to know what meaning or application it has for us today. If one is to grasp the total meaning of the entire Bible, good reference tools are a must. The congregation or hearers deserve a balanced diet of exegesis and exposition. Since the Bible is the inspired Word of God, a minister needs to be able to get into its original text, in its original context. Fortunately, there are several good reference books today that will help any minister break the original language barrier. I will attempt to list several of them in this book. In addition, I will list several works that will help the minister to make the application of the text.

There is always room for a word of caution in regard to books. General reference books about the Bible must not and cannot take the place of the Bible itself. Each reference book about the Bible must be tested by what the Bible itself says. It is important that the minister rely on the Holy Spirit first, and then, turn to his reference books lest he become too bookish. All theory and no experience makes for a superficial preacher. Books are about the most important tools of a ministers calling, provided he knows how to use them.

BIBLICAL INTRODUCTION

BRUCE, FREDERICK FYVIE, **The Books and the Parchments.** Westwood, N.J.:Fleming H. Revell Co., 1963.
This work gives an account of the original scripts and lan-

guages, the canon, text, and versions of the Bible from the beginnings of alphabetic writing to the New English Bible. A thoroughly revised and up-to-date edition of this well-known book on transmission of the Bible, including the results of the latest research and discoveries on the Dead Sea Scrolls, and many other important finds.

GEISLER, NORMAN L. and WILLIAM E. NIX. **General Introduction to the Bible, Revised and Expanded.** Chicago: Moody Press, 1986.

These noted authors have updated and expanded this work. It satisfies the exacting demands placed on any Bible introduction with precise scholarship, clarity of style, and careful organization. This balanced introduction to the Bible gives special emphasis to conservative theology and provides sharply defined answers to criticism that seeks to undermine the authority of the Bible. Holds to the inerrancy of the Bible.

MILLER, H. S. **General Biblical Introduction.** New York: The Word — Bearer Press, 1956.

In spite of its age, this book gives an excellent and thorough discussion of the inspiration of the Bible; the canonicity of the Scriptures; textual criticism and translation into English. It is a valuable work.

REFERENCE BIBLES

The New International Version Study Bible. Various Authors. Grand Rapids: Zondervan Publishing House, 1985.

This study Bible was released in 1985. It has numerous explanatory notes — more than any other study Bible. The maps and charts are frequently placed right on the text page — a unique and helpful feature. Since this study Bible was written by the translators of the New International Version of the Bible, it is clearly evangelical in theology.

THOMPSON, FRANK C., ed. **The New Chain-Reference Bible.** Indianapolis : B. B. Kirkbridge Bible Co., 1964.

Here is a life-time of study. The author worked on this project for over thirty-one years. This study Bible is a complete numerical system of chain references, analyses of books, outline studies of characters and unique charts, with pictorial maps and archaeological discoveries. This reference Bible can now be purchased with other versions. See also, C. I. Scofield, **The New Scofield Reference Bible,** Oxford University Press, 1967.

ZODHIATES, SPIRO. **Hebrew — Greek Key Study Bible.** TN : AMG Publishers, 1984.

This study Bible is gaining in popularity. Key English words are numbered within the text to Strong's Concordance numbering system for cross reference to Strong's Hebrew and Greek dictionaries and a 170 page lexicon which gives expanded treatment to key words by the author. Lengthy exegetical notes are included at the bottom of the page. This is the only key study Bible available which transliterates the original Hebrew and Greek words to the usage in the King James text, thereby providing today's readers with the exact connotation of the original writers.

BIBLE TRANSLATIONS

TAYLOR, KENNETH N. **The Living Bible.** Wheaton, IL : Tyndale House Publishers, 1971.

This paraphrased Bible can be used with caution. It is recommended that one always have a good translation handy when using The Living Bible. For when the Hebrew or Greek word is not clear, the theology of Kenneth Taylor becomes your guide.

THE HOLY BIBLE. **The New American Standard Bible.** Carol Stream, IL : Creation House, 1971.

This conservative translation is hailed by many as one of the most accurate and reliable translations presently available. It does adhere closely to the original languages, and the translation is written in a fluent and readable style according to the current English usage. This translation follows the principles used in the American Standard Verison of 1901.

THE HOLY BIBLE. **The New International Version.** Grand Rapids : Zondervan Publishing House, 1975.

The International Version of the Bible is an excellent translation from the original languages. This Bible has been written in a contemporary manner but does not tamper with the original meaning of the message for mankind. It is a completely new translation of the Holy Bible made by over a hundred scholars working directly from the best available Hebrew, Aramaic and Greek texts. Evangelical in theology.

THE HOLY BIBLE. **The New King James Version. Nashville :** Thomas Nelson and Sons, 1985.

This major new edition of the beloved 1611 version is written in modern language, and readers will discover a new and refreshing experience. This edition is the result of seven years of earnest labor by well over one hundred scholars representing the majority of English-speaking nations.

THE HOLY BIBLE. **Revised Standard Version.** New York : Thomas Nelson and Sons, 1946–52.

A good English translation for Bible study. It has many liberal tendencies in the Old Testament, but this translation can be used with profit.

BIBLE CONCORDANCES

STRONG, JAMES. **The New Strong's Exhaustive Concordance of the Bible.** New York : Thomas Nelson Publishers, 1986.

This is the only Strong's in new, easy-to-read print. Minor corrections and improvements have been made, and a new key verse comparison chart has been added which shows the most remembered and significant verses of the Bible from six major translations side by side. This concordance is more valuable than ever since many reference books have now been coded to Strong's concordance. Strong's exhaustive concordance has been one of the most valuable Bible reference tools for ministers, scholars and Bible students alike for over ninety years.

YOUNG, ROBERT. **Young's Analytical Concordance to the Bible.** New York: Thomas Nelson Publishers, 1986.

Now Young's Concordance has been corrected and updated. For the first time in this century proper name definitions have been updated and concordance text has been corrected. This unabridged edition is now crossed-referenced to Strong's Greek and Hebrew numbering system. There are over 310,000 references categorized to the Hebrew and Greek words of the original language with the literal meaning and pronunciation of the same. There are many good scholars that believe Young's is the best concordance to the Bible for Analytical purposes.

BIBLE DICTIONARIES

DOUGLAS, J. D., et al., eds. **The Illustrated Bible Dictionary.** 3 vols. Wheaton, IL: Tyndale House Publishers, 1980.

The Illustrated Bible Dictionary is probably the most up-to-date Bible dictionary available. In its range of quality scholarship and visual helpfulness it is unique among Bible reference works. Although some articles make concessions to higher criticism, it represents excellent British conservative scholarship.

UNGER, MERRILL F., ed. **Unger's Bible Dictionary.** 3d ed. Chicago: Moody Press, 1961.

This conservative work has come to be known as one of the best single-volume Bible dictionaries. The facts of history and geography of ancient Near Eastern lands as they bear upon the Bible are drawn upon extensively to make the Bible come alive.

BIBLE ENCYCLOPEDIAS

BROMILEY, G. W., et al., eds. **The International Standard Bible Encyclopedia.** Vol. I, II, III, A–P. Grand Rapids: Wm. B. Eerdmans Publishing Co., 1979.

This monumental work was first published in 1915. It has

long been considered a standard among biblical reference works. Now a new revision of this classic set is available. Combining the defining function of a dictionary with the encyclopedia's presentation of comprehensive information, the revised edition summarizes the state of knowledge about its topics and leads the reader to further resources of information and insight. Most articles are written from a conservative theology. See also, Merrill C. Tenney, **The Zondervan Pictorial Encyclopedia of the Bible,** 5 vols., Zondervan Publishing House, 1978.

ORR, JAMES, ed. **The International Standard Bible Encyclopedia.** 5 vols. Grand Rapids: Wm. B. Eerdmans Publishing Co., 1939.

This is an outstanding older work that is presently undergoing revision, but it can still be used with profit. This set represents the scholarship of hundreds of evangelical contributors from many specialized fields of biblical research. This encyclopedia includes articles on every name of a person or place mentioned in the Bible, as well as all other terms in the Bible that have theological or ethical meaning. Caution is needed with some articles since some of the contributors are not all conservative theologians.

BIBLE HANDBOOKS

HALLEY, HENRY. **Halley's Bible Handbook.** Grand Rapids: Zondervan Publishing House, 1969.

An abbreviated Bible commentary, with notes on Books of the Bible, their Historical, Geographical and Chronological background. This is an older handbook, but it can still be used with profit. For a more extensive handbook, see, **Eerdmans' Handbook to the Bible,** by David and Pat Alexander, Wm. B. Eerdmans Publishing Co., 1982.

LARSON, GARY N. **The New Unger's Bible Handbook.** Chicago: Moody Press, 1984.

This outstanding Bible handbook by Unger has now been revised and updated. It is written from the conservative viewpoint of theology. The text has been revised with hundreds of

4-color pictures added to make this volume an indispensable guide to understanding and studying the Bible.

REVELATION AND INSPIRATION

LINDSELL, HAROLD. **The Battle for the Bible.** Grand Rapids: Zondervan Publishing House, 1976.
This author pleads for evangelicals to hold to inerrancy of the Bible. For another good work see, Harold Lindsell, **The Bible In the Balance,** Zondervan Publishing House, 1979.
PACHE, RENE. **Inspiration and Authority of Scripture.** Translated by Helen I. Needham. Chicago: Moody Press, 1969.
Used as a standard text in many Christian colleges. The author holds to the complete authenticity and supernatural origin of the Bible. Evangelical.
RYRIE, CHARLES C. **What You Should Know About Inerrancy.** Chicago: Moody Press, 1982.
This work is written in a simple, clear format. Ryrie attempts to settle the issue of inerrancy from an evangelical perspective. A practical study on this important subject.
WARFIELD, BENJAMIN BRECKENRIDGE. **The Inspiration and Authority of the Bible.** Philadelphia: Presbyterian and Reformed Publishing Co., 1958.
These are vitally important essays dealing with what the Bible has to say about itself. A standard evangelical work. For another older work, see also, E. J. Young, **Thy Word is Truth,** Wm. B. Eerdmans Publishing Co., 1957.

SCIENCE AND THE BIBLE

CRISWELL, WALLIE AMOS. **Did Man Just Happen?** Grand Rapids: Zondervan Publishing House, 1957.
This volume contains some excellent preaching material. Criswell is an outstanding expository preacher. Here is a great work by an evangelical Southern Baptist pastor.

CUSTANCE, ARTHUR C. **The Doorway Papers.** 10 vols. Grand Rapids: Zondervan Publishing House, 1975.

These papers are practical and extensive in the study of Science and the Bible. A valuable set for those who want to do some serious study in this important subject.

MORRIS, HENRY MADISON. **Studies in the Bible and Science.** Grand Rapids: Baker Book House, 1966.

One of the best authorities on the Bible and Science today. This author has other excellent books on this subject that will prove to be both practical and helpful.

RAMM, BERNARD LAWRENCE. **The Christian View of Science and Scripture.** Grand Rapids: Wm. B. Eerdmans Publishing Co., 1954.

An invaluable work for the study of Science and the Bible, but it should be used with caution in some areas. "The best single volume, from a conservative standpoint, that has thus far appeared, is the work by Dr. Bernard Ramm, The Christian View of Science and the Scriptures. . . ." — Dr. Wilber M. Smith.

BIBLICAL INTERPRETATION: HERMENEUTICS

MICKELSEN, A. B. **Interpreting the Bible.** Grand Rapids: Wm. B. Eerdmans Publishing Co., 1963.

An evangelical comprehensive text that seeks to cover every aspect of hermeneutics in the light of contemporary issues. Overlooks some problems facing expositors today, but the work has some excellent material. See also, Henry A. Virkler, **Hermeneutics: Principles and Processes of Biblical Interpretation,** Baker Book House, 1981.

RAMM, BERNARD LAWRENCE. **Protestant Biblical Interpretation.** 3d rev. ed. Grand Rapids: Baker Book House, 1970.

". . . this book ought to be in the hands of all who intend to do serious work in the field of hermeneutics." — Dr. Wilber M. Smith.

TERRY, MILTON SPENCE. **Biblical Hermeneutics.** Grand Rapids: Zondervan Publishing House, 1968.

Here is a large comprehensive work in the area of Biblical Interpretation. Thoroughly conservative with excellent help for the serious student of Hermeneutics. First published in 1883.

BIBLICAL TYPOLOGY

FAIRBAIRN, PATRICK. **The Typology of Scripture.** 5th ed. Grand Rapids: Zondervan Publishing House, 1963.

A classic reprint from the 1900 edition. The most conclusive evangelical work on typology. A thorough study of the pictures of redemption and the redeemer which God has given us in the Old Testament as well as the principles for the interpretation of types.

HABERSHON, ADA RUTH. **Study of the Types.** Grand Rapids: Kregel Publications, 1961.

This book while not dealing exclusively with the Levitical types and offerings does include them. Full of useful hints, thoughts and illustrations for the minister.

BIBLICAL ARCHAEOLOGY

BLAIKLOCK, E. M. AND R. K. HARRISON. eds. **The New International Dictionary of Biblical Archaeology.** Grand Rapids: Zondervan Publishing House, 1984.

More than 800 articles discuss the whole range of Biblical Archaeology in a definitive survey of the subject. Photos (in color as well as black-and-white), charts, maps and other aids complement the text. A very helpful reference book on this subject.

UNGER, MERRILL F. **Archaeology and the Old Testament.** Grand Rapids: Zondervan Publishing House, 1960.

Unger is an excellent writer of many Old Testament Books. This study is extremely practical. ". . . the best conservative introductory work on this area of study." — Dr. Wilber M. Smith.

————. **Archaeology and the New Testament.** Grand Rapids: Zondervan Publishing House, 1970.
This is a good comprehensive survey suitable for either beginners or advanced readers. The sections on the historical background enhance the value of this work.

BIBLE GEOGRAPHY

AHARONI, YOHANAN, AND MICHAEL AVI YONAH. **The Macmillan Bible Atlas.** Revised ed. New York: Macmillan Company, 1977.
Now held to be the standard work on the Old Testament and New Testament times. Very informative and loaded with information on Biblical Geography.

PFEIFFER, CHARLES FRANKLIN, ed. **Baker's Bible Atlas.** Grand Rapids: Baker Book House, 1961. Revised ed., 1973.
A Bible geography containing 26 colored maps, 75 photographs to illustrate, numerous black-and-white maps. Emphasis on geography follows the Scriptural narrative from Genesis through Revelation. Evangelical. See also, C. F. Pfeiffer, and Howard F. Vos, eds., **Wycliff Historical Geography of Bible Lands,** Moody Press, 1967.

THOMPSON, WILLIAM MCCLURE. **The Land and the Book.** Grand Rapids: Baker Book House, 1966.
A classic first published in 1880. Still practical and helpful to the modern student. This is an abridgement of the older three volume edition.

TURNER, GEORGE ALLEN. **Historical Geography of the Holy Land.** Grand Rapids: Baker Book House, 1973.
An invaluable aid to Bible study as it provides needed historical and geographical background for the serious student.

BIBLE HISTORY

BRUCE, FREDERICK FYVIE. **New Testament History.** New York: Thomas Nelson and Sons, 1971.

The author presents an excellent background to New Testament history. Most of the time, Bruce is conservative in his theology. A very helpful standard work.

EDERSHEIM, ALFRED. **Bible History.** Grand Rapids: Wm. B. Eerdmans Publishing Co., 1972.

This classic work was originally published in 1876–1887, in seven volumes. It went through several editions, some of which were bound in four volumes, and later in two volumes. The present edition is an important reprint of that which appeared in 1890, complete and unabridged, containing all seven volumes, bound between two covers. It covers the history of Israel from before the Flood to the time of the Babylonian captivity. See also, Charles F. Pfeiffer, **Old Tesament History,** Baker Book House, 1973.

JOSEPHUS, FLAVIUS. **Complete Works of Josephus.** Translated by William Whiston. Grand Rapids: Kregel Publications, 1963.

A complete, accurate documentation of Jewish history. It contains the first known reference to Jesus Christ by a secular historian. A classic for understanding Jewish culture and thinking.

KITTO, JOHN. **Kitto's Daily Bible Illustrations.** 2 vols. Grand Rapids: Kregel Publications, 1985.

This classic work has now been reprinted. Kitto was a tremendous expositor, providing the minister with several illustrations of several texts of Scripture. Practical.

WOOD, LEON JAMES. **A Survey of Israel's History.** Grand Rapids: Zondervan Publishing House, 1970.

A practical work written from an evangelical viewpoint treating the highlights of Israel's History. Maps, charts, and diagrams combine with the text to offer a thorough understanding of this subject.

BIBLE MANNERS AND CUSTOMS

COLEMAN, WILLIAM L. **Today's Handbook of Bible Times and Customs.** Minneapolis: Bethany House Publishers, 1984.

This recent work incorporates all recent archaeological findings and avoids overly technical material. Pastors and Bible students will find this handbook a reliable reference work. Well illustrated.

WIGHT, FRED H. **The New Manners and Customs of Bible Lands.** Chicago: Moody Press, 1986.

This newly revised edition by Ralph Gower is one of the best works on manners and customs of Bible lands. Much light is shed upon many puzzling Bible Word pictures in this book. All ministers will welcome this edition to their own personal library.

General Books About the Bible and Commentaries

More commentaries and other books about the Bible are now appearing than any one minister will ever be able to read in his entire lifetime. Only after one has exhausted other resources, should they turn to a commentary. If you have done your exegesis well, or discovered what the text means, then it is time to look into a good commentary. Looking into a commentary first could make you a parrot rather than a Bible student. The temptation for all minister's is to depend upon secondary sources too much for preaching material. It is only after you have done your best to understand the text, that you are even qualified to evaluate the findings in a commentary.

How can you best evaluate a commentary? The author should be accurate and balanced in his exposition before giving place to application. You will never be able to agree with every authors exposition or application. Most likely, if it is a good commentary, you will be in basic agreement. But never pass up a good commentary just because you cannot agree with all of his conclusions or all his theology. On the other hand, when one commentator advances an idea totally rejected by others, be cautious! Not always, but generally speaking, there is a lot of merit in a consensus of opinion.

You can also evaluate a commentary by comparing one against the other. This is why it is important to have more than one commentary on every book of the Bible. If you have more than one commentary, it will protect you from depending on one author for all of your conclusions. Because commentaries are usually one person's interpretation of Scripture, knowledge of the author's theological view is more important than for other biblical reference works. It is important to choose wisely in one's selection of commentaries.

Then, there are differences in respect to every minister's background and reading level. Some are comfortable with the original languages and some are not. In this section, the author will not recommend highly technical volumes or books that require a knowledge of the original languages. It is interesting to note that only 10% of those who begin to study Greek ever master the language after their formal training. It is even worse for those who study Hebrew. Only 1% ever master that language after their formal training. Since the majority of minister's do not master the original Bible languages, the author will not be recommending highly technical commentaries or technical books about the Bible.

The most important thing to keep in mind is balance in the selection of a good commentary. At times, as many as five commentaries on one book of the Bible will be recommended, because each commentary has its own unique objective. Some commentaries may be devotional, homiletical, expositional, exegetical, or critical. Read the comments carefully before you select, so that you will acquire a balance for each book of the Bible. Unlike other books that have been written about the minister's library, the author will only recommend books that are basically evangelical and be very specific as to what books one should purchase.

This section will also include works of shorter biblical passages on the Old and New Testament. For example, books on the Ten Commandments and the Tabernacle will be found under the Book of Exodus. The same will be true for short biblical passages on the New Testament. Books on the Lord's Prayer or the Sermon on the Mount can be located under the Gospel of Matthew. In addition, expositions on various Bible characters will be located in their Biblical placement for easy reference.

This author feels that a one-volume commentary is not satisfactory for the average minister. If you are going to purchase a commentary on the entire Bible, it is wise to choose a set that has been written by different authors. There are very few exceptions to this rule, but there are a few. Of course, the best commentaries are those written by individual authors on a certain book of the Bible. These author's have done their homework and a good commentary or a good book about the Bible is every bit as much a gift to the preacher as is a good sermon, good lectures on tapes, or a good counselor.

BOOKS ON THE OLD TESTAMENT
OLD TESTAMENT BIBLE INTRODUCTIONS

ARCHER, GLEASON LEONARD, JR. **A Survey of Old Testament Introduction.** Chicago: Moody Press, 1964.

Archer's purpose is to furnish a simple and usable text for the instruction of college and seminary students who have no previous training in Old Testament criticism. This work takes an excellent conservative approach to the Old Testament. For a more comprehensive study, see also, Roland K. Harrison, **Introduction to the Old Testament,** Wm. B. Eerdmans Publishing Co., 1966.

PURKISER, W. T. **Exploring the Old Testament.** Kansas City, MO.: Beacon Hill Press, 1955.

An important work from an Arminian/Wesleyan view of theology. It is based on the King James Version of the Bible, tracing the literature and history of the Hebrew nation in an easy to follow outline form. Evangelical.

YOUNG, EDWARD JOSEPH. **An Introduction to the Old Testament.** rev. ed. Grand Rapids: Wm. B. Eerdmans Publishing Co., 1960.

"It is a must on the list of every man in this country seriously interested in the interpretation of the Old Testament."— Dr. Wilber M. Smith. For another helpful older work, see also, Merrill F. Unger's, **Introductory Guide to the Old Testament,** Zondervan Publishing House, 1951.

OLD TESTAMENT THEOLOGY

KAISER, WALTER C., JR. **Toward an Old Testament Theology.** Grand Rapids: Zondervan Publishing House, 1978.

A much needed recent work on Old Testament biblical theology. The author approaches this subject from a conservative view of theology.

PAYNE, JOHN BARTON. **The Theology of the Older Testament.** Grand Rapids: Zondervan Publishing House, 1962.

A most helpful volume in Old Testament theology, from a

evangelical viewpoint. See also, the older classic work by Gustav F. Oehler, **Theology of the Old Testament,** Klock and Klock Publishers, 1984.

OLD TESTAMENT WORD STUDIES

GIRDLESTONE, ROBERT BAKER. **Girdlestone's Synonyms of the Old Testament.** 3d ed. Grand Rapids: Baker Book House, 1984.

The translation work, newly revised text, introduction, and especially the numerical apparatus make this work widely useful for the first time to pastors and Bible students without knowledge of Hebrew. This classic work is now numerically coded to Strong's Exhaustive Concordance.

HARRIS, ROBERT LAIRD; GLEASON LEONARD ARCHER, JR., AND BRUCE KENNETH WALTKE, eds. **Theological Wordbook of the Old Testament.** 2 vols. Chicago: Moody Press, 1980.

Every pastor can use this work in sermon preparation without knowledge of the Hebrew language. This set is uniquely tied to Strong's Exhaustive Concordance. This extensive work includes discussions of every Hebrew word of theological significance in the O. T., plus brief definitions of all other words found in the Brown, Driver, and Briggs Hebrew Lexicon. There is also a special section of Aramaic words used in the O. T.

RICHARDS, LAWRENCE O. **Expository Dictionary of Bible Words.** Grand Rapids: Zondervan Publishing House, 1985.

A valuable reference tool for the minister or any serious student of Scripture. It is highly readable and a concise guideline for understanding many words in the Bible. Gives a summary of the meanings of nearly 1,500 English Bible words as they are used in both the Old and New Testaments.

UNGER, MERRILL F., AND WILLIAM WHITE, JR., eds. **An Expository Dictionary of Biblical Words.** Nashville: Thomas Nelson Publishers, 1985.

This volume combines the contents of Vine's Expository

Dictionary of N. T. Word and the Expository Dictionary of the O. T. by Unger and White. It is more comprehensive in covering O. T. words than Vine's O. T. and N. T. Words Studies, due to the brevity of Vine's O. T. Word Studies. In addition, this new revised edition has each word now coded to Strong's Concordance and indices to the B-D-B lexicon and the Bauer-Arndt-Gingrich Greek lexicon are included. The most comprehensive expository dictionary available anywhere.

WILSON WILLIAM. **Old Testament Word Studies.** Grand Rapids: Kregel Publications, 1978.

Wilson's is a valuable tool for both the Hebrew student and those who do not have a working knowledge of the language, offering an aid for the understanding of word meanings and help in understanding difficult passages. It is both an exhaustive dictionary and a concordance in that significant English words translated from more than one original Hebrew word have a listing of major Scripture references coded to each original Hebrew word used. The book is arranged in English alphabetical order, giving every Hebrew word with its literal English meaning.

OLD TESTAMENT LANGUAGE TOOLS

GESENIUS, FRIEDRICH HEINRICH WILHELM. **The New Brown—Driver Briggs Hebrew Aramaic Lexicon.** Massachusetts: Hendrickson Publishers, 1985.

The classic Work "B—D—B" has been improved in this revision of the most complete 1907 edition, making it by far the most useful Hebrew/Aramaic lexicon available to the English-speaking student. In addition, this work is coded to the Strong's Concordance numbering system, thus allowing the novice Hebrew student and even students and pastors who do not know Hebrew ready access to this valuable tool.

GREEN, JAY P. **The Interlinear Old Testament.** 3 vols. Massachusetts: Hendrickson Publishers, 1986.

Now students and pastors who want to work with the Hebrew language can do so with this outstanding set. Every Old Testament word is keyed to Strong's Concordance numbering system. This work supplies a literal English translation for each Hebrew word. Any person can now read the original text without losing valuable time to look up words in a Hebrew lexicon. Since only a small minority of pastors and students retain an easy ready comprehension of the Hebrew text, The Interlinear Old Testament will be a welcome language tool.

WIGRAM, GEORGE W. **The New Englishman's Hebrew-Aramaic Concordance.** Massachusetts: Hendrickson Publishers, 1985.

The New Englishman's Hebrew-Aramaic Concordance is an improved edition of the standard reference work first issued in 1843 entitled **The Englishman's Hebrew and Chaldee Concordance of the Old Testament.** Every Hebrew and Aramaic word of the Old Testament is listed in (Hebrew) alphabetical order along with a brief rendering in English of every verse in the Old Testament in which that Hebrew-Aramaic word appears. Best of all, each word is coded to Strong's Concordance thus allowing even those who do not know Hebrew the opportunity to utilize this work. The page numbers to the NEW Brown-Driver-Briggs Hebrew-Aramaic Lexicon are also included with each entry, making reference to this important reference work possible for those who do not know Hebrew and easier for those who do.

COMMENTARIES ON THE ENTIRE BIBLE

CLARKE, ADAM. **Clarke's Commentary.** 3 vols. New York: Abingdon-Cokesbury Press, reprint.

Now in three double volumes. "Prince of Commentators" and a master linguist. This set is a classic written from an Arminian/Wesleyan viewpoint.

GAEBELEIN, F. E., **The Expositor's Bible Commentary.** 12 vols. Grand Rapids: Zondervan Publishing House, 1979.

This work brings together an international team of Seventy-Eight authors representing the best evangelical scholarship in the English-speaking world. They are committed to the divine inspiration, complete trustworthiness, and full authority of Scripture. This team of scholars represent theological and ecclesiastical traditions as diverse as Calvinist and Arminian, Anglican, Mennonite, and Baptist. This recent work is based on the New International Version of the Bible.

HENRY, MATTHEW. **Commentary on the Whole Bible.** 6 vols. Westwood, N. J.: Fleming H. Revell, reprint.

One of the better devotional commentaries on the Bible. ". . . it will remain in the very first class as long as the Christian Church is on earth."—Dr. Wilber M. Smith.

LANGE, JOHN PETER, **Commentary on the Holy Scriptures.** 12 vols. Michigan: Zondervan Publishing House, 1969.

One of the most used commentaries on the whole Bible. This work is critical, doctrinal and homiletical in content with inexhaustible ideas for preachers. Lange was one of the greatest scholars of his day. Particularly helpful on the OT!

MACLAREN, ALEXANDER, **Expositions of Holy Scripture.** 17 vols. Grand Rapids: Baker Book House, reprint.

Here is expository preaching at its best. Everyone that is devoting his life to preaching will want this set. ". . . so long as preachers care to teach from the Scriptures they will find their best guide and help in him."—Dr. Wilber M. Smith.

The Pulpit Commentary. Edited by H. D. Spence and Joseph S. Exell. 23 vols. Grand Rapids: Wm. B. Eerdmans Publishing Co., 1963.

This is one of the largest homiletical commentary sets of its kind. It has been widely used by thousands of preachers and Bible students. The format of this work is geared specifically for sermon preparation and study. A classic reference work by various authors. For a more up-to-date homiletical commentary, see, Lloyd J. Ogilvie, **The Communicator's Commentary,** 12 vols., Word Books, 1982.

The Wesleyan Bible Commentary. 6 vols. Edited by Charles W. Carter, Ralph Earle, and W. Ralph Thompson. Massachusetts: Hendrickson Publishers, Inc., 1986.

This work was first published in the 1960's and is cast in the framework of contemporary evangelical Wesleyan Bible scholarship. The commentary is expositional, practical, homiletical and devotional. It was the first multi-volume commenting on the entire Bible by a distinguished community of Wesleyan scholars, representing nine evangelical denominations. Extremely valuable from an Arminian viewpoint of theology. For another Arminian/Wesleyan commentary, see also, H. F. Harper, **Beacon Bible Commentary,** 10 vols., Beacon Hill Press, 1964–1969.

COMMENTARIES ON THE ENTIRE OLD TESTAMENT

KEIL, JOHANN KARL FRIEDRICH AND FRANZ JULIUS DELITZSCH. **Biblical Commentary on the Old Testament.** 10 vols. Grand Rapids: Wm. B. Eerdmans Publishing Co., reprint.

This classic set was first published in the 1800's. But the best Commentary isn't always the latest. It is this author's experience that some of the older commentaries can still be the best. Age plays only a minor role when evaluating the quality of a good commentary. This work is still a rich source of information for any minister with or without a knowledge of the Hebrew language. It is written from a conservative view of theology.

Tyndale Old Testament Commentaries. Edited by Donald J. Wiseman. 16 vols. Downers Grove, IL.: Inter-Varsity Press, 1980.

The aim of this series is to provide a handy, up-to-date commentary on each book of the Old Testament, with the primary emphasis on exegesis. This work emphasizes a passage-by-passage exegesis and avoids undue technicalities. It will provide the serious reader of the Bible with practical tools for interpretation and explanation. Most of the time, the authors are evangelical in their theology. Some volumes should be used with caution.

INDIVIDUAL COMMENTARIES ON
OLD TESTAMENT BOOKS
THE PENTATEUCH

ALLIS, OSWALD T. **The Five Books of Moses.** 2d ed. Philadelphia: Presbyterian and Reformed Publishing Co., 1949.

A thorough refutation of the J,E,P,D theory. Dr. Allis not only points out the critics' inconsistency, but he also shows that their methods cannot be applied to other pieces of literature written by one author without similar results. The author gives forth the meaning of the text of Genesis, Exodus, Leviticus, Numbers and Deuteronomy; and sets it forth in non-technical language.

LIVINGSTONE, GEORGE HERBERT. **The Pentateuch in Its Cultural Environment.** Grand Rapids: Baker Book House, 1974.

This recent work does an excellent job of giving helpful background information on the Pentateuch. A valuable contribution to this area of study.

MACKINTOSH, CHARLES H. **Genesis to Deuteronomy: Notes on the Pentateuch.** New Jersey: Loizeaux Brothers, 1974.

These studies were written by a Plymouth Brethren. They are devotional and typological. Good reading, but one has to watch out for some extremes in typology. Strongly recommended by D. L. Moody. Formerly in six volumes.

MEYER, FREDERICK BROTHERTON. **The Five Books of Moses.** London: Marshall, Morgan and Scott, 1955.

A very helpful devotional and homiletical commentary on the Pentateuch. This work contains good sermon material on these important books of the Old Testament.

NEWELL, WILLIAM R. **Studies in the Pentateuch.** Grand Rapids: Kregel Publications, 1983.

This concise work draws out spiritual truths from the books of the Pentateuch. It also offers valuable facts and excellent material helps for sermon preparation.

THOMAS, W. H. GRIFFITH. **Through the Pentateuch.** Grand Rapids: Kregel Publications, 1985.

These valuable notes take the form of a connected commentary on the Pentateuch. A helpful introduction to each book plus the excellent homiletical material will give the minister devotional insights into the Pentateuchal writings. Evangelical.

BIBLE CHARACTERS ON THE PENTATEUCH

BLAIKIE, WILLIAM GARDEN. **Heroes of Israel.** Minneapolis: Klock and Klock Christian Publishers, 1983.

This volume covers the Bible characters mentioned in the Book of Genesis and the narrative parts of Exodus and Numbers. The graphic pen-portraits contained within this work will be welcomed by ministers preaching on Bible characters.

HAMILTON, JAMES. **Moses, the Man of God.** Minneapolis: Klock and Klock Christian Publishers, 1985.

This delightful handling of the life of Moses will enlighten any minister or Bible student. This valuable classic reprint will prove invaluable to the minister's library.

KIRK, THOMAS. **The Life of Joseph.** Minneapolis: Klock and Klock Christian Publishers, 1985.

This is an excellent treatment of the great life of Joseph. Kirk shows diligent research, painstaking detail and considerable insight in these studies. The homiletical helps are abundant in this volume.

MEYER, FREDERICK BROTHERTON. **Abraham: The Obedience of Faith.** London: Marshall, Morgan and Scott, 1953.

A very helpful devotional work on the life of Abraham. It will aid any minister in their preaching on this great Bible character of faith.

———. **Moses, the Servant of God.** London: Marshall, Morgan and Scott, 1953.

Once again, this author demonstrates his ability to make Bible characters come alive. This devotional work will give the minister several ideas for preaching on the life of Moses.

―――――. **Israel. A Prince with God.** London: Marshall, Morgan and Scott, 1909.

These older devotional studies on the life of Jacob are valuable. People enjoy preaching on Bible characters. Meyer will aid any minister in his sermon preparation on the life of Jacob.

―――――. **Joseph: Beloved, Hated, Exalted.** London: Marshall, Morgan and Scott, 1955.

The life of Joseph is very important for personal study. Meyer gives much perceptive insight into the life of this great Bible character. A devotional work.

TAYLOR, WILLIAM MACKERGO. **Joseph the Prime Minister.** Grand Rapids: Baker Book House, 1961.

This author was an outstanding expository preacher. He masters the life of Joseph in this intriging study. This is a devotional and expositional study on this Bible character.

―――――. **Moses: The Law Giver.** Grand Rapids: Baker Book House, 1961.

These practical expositions on the life of Moses are excellent examples of expository preaching. You will want to purchase all of Taylor's works on Bible characters.

GENESIS

BUSH, GEORGE. **Notes on Genesis.** 2 vols. in 1. Minneapolis: The James Family, 1979.

This volume contains rich expository notes based upon the original text. Of practical value to the pastor with little or no knowledge of Hebrew.

CANDLISH, ROBERT SMITH. **Studies in Genesis.** Grand Rapids: Kregel Publications, 1979.

This is a very important classic work on Genesis. It has a treasure-house of sermon suggestions and teachings. These are expository messages, thoroughly conservative, rich in devotional emphasis and contain many theological discussions that will be of special value to ministers. Doctrinal and biographical.

DAVIS, JOHN JAMES. **Paradise to Prison: Studies in Genesis.** Grand Rapids: Baker Book House, 1975.

A superior textbook and complete study guide on the Book of Genesis interwoven with maps, photos, and vivid text. This is a good historical survey, making use of the latest archaelogical findings. Evangelical in theology.

JUKES, ANDREW. **Types in Genesis.** Grand Rapids: Kregel Publications, 1981.

A classic reprint on typology as revealed in the Book of Genesis. Here is a book that contains much spiritual warmth and depth.

LEUPOLD, HERBERT CARL. **Exposition of Genesis.** 2 vols. Grand Rapids: Baker Book House, 1942.

Extremely well done by an Evangelical Lutheran scholar. "I believe it is the most important commentary on Genesis that has ever been published by an American scholar."—Dr. Wilber M. Smith.

MORRIS, HENRY M. **The Genesis Record.** Grand Rapids: Baker Book House, 1985.

Although there are several commentaries on Genesis in print, this is the only work on the complete Book of Genesis written by a creation scientist. It is written as a narrative devotional exposition rather than a critical verse-by-verse analysis. The author makes practical application of the Genesis account to the Christian life. Conservative.

PINK, ARTHUR WALKINGTON. **Gleaning in Genesis.** Chicago: Moody Press, 1981.

This commentary develops the Book of Exodus around the theme of redemption, presenting the need of redemption, the might of the Redeemer, the character of redemption, the duty of the redeemed, and the provisions made for failure.

STRAHAN, JAMES. **Hebrew Ideals in Genesis.** Grand Rapids: Kregel Publications, 1982.

A classic reprint dealing with the heart and spirit of the people and events in Genesis. Then these Hebrew ideals are related to the ideals of life today. This is a valuable character study highly recommended by Dr. Wilber M. Smith.

THOMAS, WILLIAM HENRY GRIFFITH. **A Devotional**

Commentary. Grand Rapids: Wm. B. Eerdmans Publishing Co., 1946.

A highly recommended devotional commentary on Genesis. This author has mastered all the relevant literature pertaining to this Book, making it truly sound in biblical scholarship. Evangelical.

YOUNG, EDWARD JOSEPH. **Studies in Genesis One.** Philadelphia: Presbyterian and Reformed Publishing Co., 1964.

A masterful exposition on Genesis 1, giving a thorough discussion of the creation account. Conservative and expository.

————. **Genesis Three. A Devotional and Expository Study.** London: Banner of Truth Trust, 1966.

This book contains some of the best exegetical work on Genesis 3 to be found anywhere. In this good effort from Dr. Young, he shows Adam's historicity to be absolutely undeniable.

WHITCOMB, JOHN CLEMENT, JR., and HENRY M. MORRIS. **The Genesis Flood.** Philadelphia: Presbyterian and Reformed Publishing Co., 1962.

A very stimulating book, helping to understand questions which scientist raise against the Bible. Many times these scientists are proven to be wrong. The authors hold to a universal flood. They then proceed to examine the geological data which bear on the subject and show that it can be brought into harmony with the Biblical account without weakening the teaching of Scripture or denying the facts of science.

EXODUS

ALFORD, HENRY. **The Book of Genesis, and Part of the Book of Exodus.** Minneapolis: Klock and Klock Christian Publishers, 1979.

This work is a reprint, by an outstanding biblical writer. You have to watch some of his views of the Documentary Hypothesis of the Old Testament.

BUSH, GEORGE. **Notes on Exodus.** Minneapolis: The James Family, 1979.

Preachers will find these expository studies helpful in sermon preparation. The author gives a careful evaluation of the Hebrew text. Of practical value to the preacher with little or no knowledge of Hebrew.

DAVIS, JOHN JAMES. **Moses and the Gods of Egypt. Old Testament Studies.** Grand Rapids: Baker Book House, 1972.

This is a work in the Studies of the Book of Exodus written in the light of recent archaeological and historical research. Evangelical in theology.

MEYER, FREDERICK BROTHERTON. **Devotional Commentary on Exodus.** Grand Rapids: Kregel Publications, 1983.

This commentary is both devotional and expositional. It will be extremely helpful in sermon application. Meyer was a leading British Baptist preacher in his time.

MURPHY, JAMES GRACEY. **A Critical and Exegetical Commentary on the Book of Exodus.** Minneapolis: Klock and Klock Christian Publishers, 1980.

Murphy was an Irish Presbyterian scholar of the 19th century. He had a keen knowledge of the Hebrew language. This work is a treasure in spite of its age. It will be useful to all expositors in sermon preparation. See also, **The Book of Exodus.** The Expositor's Bible, Baker Book House, reprint.

PINK, ARTHUR W. **Gleanings in Exodus.** Chicago: Moody Press, 1972.

Heavily typological, but still helpful on the practical thoughts of Exodus. Pink is a little extreme in his Calvinistic theology but he always has some great devotional thoughts.

THE TEN COMMANDMENTS

BARCLAY, WILLIAM. **The Ten Commandments for Today.** New York: Pyramid Publications, 1977.

A significant expositional work on the Decalogue. Be careful of the liberal theology of this author. The background material is extremely helpful.

CHAPPELL, CLOVIS GILLHAM. **Ten Rules for Living.** New York: Abingdon Press, 1938.

This author gives some extremely practical ideas for preparing messages on the Ten Commandments. Chappell preaches clearly and illustrates each major thought.

MORGAN, GEORGE CAMPBELL. **The Ten Commandments.** New York: Fleming H. Revell, Co., n.d.
"Morgan wrote one of the most remarkable books on the Decalogue."—Dr. Wilber M. Smith. A most practical and expositional work on this study.

THE TABERNACLE

HALDEMAN, I. M. **Tabernacle, Priesthood and the Offerings.** New York: Fleming H. Revell, Co., n.d.
A valuable, practical exposition of the verses in Exodus dealing with the Tabernacle Priesthood and the Offerings. See also, James Strong, **Tabernacle of Israel,** Kregel Publications, 1986.

SOLTAU, HENRY W. **The Tabernacle, the Priesthood and the Offerings.** Harrisburg, Penn.: Christian Publications, n.d.
A classic comprehensive study unfolding the beauties and glories of the Lord Jesus Christ as portrayed in the Jewish Ritual. This work avoids extreme and fanciful spiritualization often found in many books on typology. Contains a wealth of direct practical teaching regarding the daily life of the Christian and the maintenance of communion with God.

————. **The Holy Vessels and Furniture of the Tabernacle.** Grand Rapids: Kregel Publications, 1970.
An older work dealing the vessels and furniture of the Tabernacle. Very helpful exposition giving the most correct delineation from Scripture of the contents of the Tabernacle that has ever appeared. The furniture and vessels used in the Tabernacle are all treated in their typical significance for the believers instruction and the riches of the Old Testament economy are unfolded for the New Testament saint.

LEVITICUS

BONAR, ANDREW ALEXANDER. **A Commentary on the Book of Leviticus.** Reprint. Grand Rapids: Zondervan Publishing House, 1959.

A classic devotional commentary on one of the least read and understood books of the Bible. Unexcelled in his approach to typical analogy. Most helpful to any minister in his study on Leviticus.

BUSH, GEORGE. **Notes on Leviticus.** Minneapolis: James and Klock Publishing Co., 1976.

This older work shows the beauty of God's Redemption as revealed in the Book of Leviticus. These are some of the best notes on Leviticus in print today.

KELLOGG, SAMUEL HENRY. **The Book of Leviticus.** Minneapolis: Klock and Klock Christian Publishers, 1982.

An outstanding commentary on Leviticus. This older classic book is included in the Expositor's Bible. In this work, Kellogg staunchly defends Mosaic authorship and ably treats Jewish ceremonial law in all its aspects.

JUKES, ANDREW JOHN. **The Law of the Offerings.** Grand Rapids: Kregel Publications, 1980.

This work is a classic on the typological significance of the offerings mentioned in Leviticus, showing how each clearly points to some particular aspect of the redemptive work of Christ. The author clearly defines the significance of this Judeo-Religious rite and its application to the New Testament Church.

SEISS, JOSEPH. **Gospel in Leviticus.** Grand Rapids: Kregel Publications, 1981.

This classic book was out-of-print for many years. In this standard evangelical work on Leviticus, the author has been able to clearly define and explain how the book of Leviticus points forward to Christ. He gives the symbolism of the book of Leviticus new meaning. The work is critical, doctrinal, practical, and expository. See also, Johann H. Kurtz, **Sacrificial Worship in the Old Testament,** Klock and Klock Christian Publishers, 1980.

WENHAM, GORDON J. **The Book of Leviticus.** New International Commentary on the Old Testament. Grand Rapids: Wm. B. Eerdmans Publishing Co., 1979.

A recent work of exposition by an evangelical writer. Much of its value lies in its recent scholarship. The writer provides a good balance of both technical information and devotional material.

NUMBERS

BUSH, GEORGE. **Notes, Critical and Practical on the Book of Numbers.** Minneapolis: James and Klock Christian Publishers, 1977.

One does not have to have a knowledge of Hebrew to use this work. In spite of its age, this book has many relevant comments on the Book of Numbers.

HESLOP, WILLIAM H. **Nuggets from Numbers.** Grand Rapids: Kregel Publications, 1984.

This concise work unfolds several Biblical truths from the Book of Numbers. Heslop has a series of seven other helpful books on the Old Testament. Evangelical.

JENSEN, IRVING LESTER. **Numbers: Journey to God's Rest Land.** Chicago: Moody Press, 1964.

This brief work is based on the English text, instead of the exegetical text. It is written in a very clear style. Practical and evangelical.

NOORDTZIJ, A. **Numbers.** The Bible Student's Commentary. Grand Rapids: Zondervan Publishing House, 1983.

This commentary is the fourth volume in a series translating the Dutch Korte Verklaring. The author gives a good understanding of the principles of the atonement and holiness found in Leviticus. A highly regarded work for its practical exegetical insights. This book is a verse-by-verse explanation of the text. Evangelical.

WAGNER, GEORGE. **Practical Truths from Israel's Wanderings.** Grand Rapids: Kregel Publications, 1985.

The author draws out similarities between Israel's wanderings in the wilderness and a Christian's pilgrimage through life. A classic reprint of over 384 pages.

DEUTERONOMY

CRAIGIE, PETER C. **The Book of Deuteronomy.** New International Commentary on the Old Testament. Grand Rapids: Wm. B. Erdmans Publishing Co., 1977.

This book contains over 400 pages on the very important Book of Deuteronomy. The author wrote in a scholarly style with practical insights to the text. He defends the integrity of Moses' writings. Evangelical.

CUMMINGS, JOHN. **Deuteronomy.** Minneapolis: Klock and Klock Christian Publishers, 1984.

This book is the best known of Dr. Cummings' more than 200 expositions of many of the books of the Bible. It is a classic reprint of an 1856 edition, containing homely expositions rather than a verse-by-verse commentary. The author furnishes a constant flow of spiritual applications to the text.

RIDDERBOS, HERMAN N. **Deuteronomy.** The Bible Student's Commentary. Grand Rapids: Zondervan Publishing House, 1985.

This work is another in a series from the Dutch Reformed tradition. A commentary highly regarded for its exegetical insights and its verse-by-verse explanation of the text. Generally, evangelical in theology.

THE HISTORICAL BOOKS

DAVIS, JOHN JAMES AND JOHN CLEMENT WHITCOMB, JR. **A History of Israel from Conquest to Exile.** Grand Rapids: Baker Book House, 1980.

An excellent study covering Israel's history from the period of Joshua and the Judges to the Babylonian exile. This work makes the best use of the latest archaeological findings and deals with all the difficult problems in the Books of Joshua, Judges, and Ruth.

GARSTANG, JOHN. **Joshua–Judges: Foundations of Bible History.** Grand Rapids: Kregel Publications, 1985.

This is an older work that deals with the text along with several color maps, charts and photographs accurately reveal the historical context and archeological finds for the Books of Joshua and Judges. Be cautious since the author adheres to the documentary hypothesis theory.

MEYER, FREDERICK B. **Choice Notes on Joshua-Second Kings.** Grand Rapids: Kregel Publications, 1985.

The design of this book is to make understandable, accessible notes from the books of Joshua to 2 Kings. This work will bring new understanding, insight and challenge. A chapter by chapter study. Devotional.

NEWELL, W. R. **Studies in Joshua–Job.** Grand Rapids: Kregel Publications, 1983.

Popular studies with an excellent synopsis of the historical books. It is written in a clear manner and surveys each book giving key ideas and insight.

BIBLE CHARACTERS ON THE HISTORICAL BOOKS

BLAIKIE, WILLIAM GARDEN. **David, King of Israel.** Minneapolis: Klock and Klock Christian Publishers, 1982.

Do not confuse this work with the author's individual commentaries on the Old Testament. This is a valuable work on the life of David. At one time, this book was difficult to find.

DEAN, WILLIAM JOHN AND THOMAS KIRK. **Studies in the First Book of Samuel.** Minneapolis: Klock and Klock Christian Publishers, 1984.

These studies are the combination of two older classic works, Deane's **Samuel and Saul: Their Lives and Times** and Kirk's **Saul: First King of Israel.** Devotional and practical.

KRUMMACHER, FREDERICK WILLIAM. **David the King of Israel.** Minneapolis: Klock and Klock Christian Publishers, 1985.

The minister will find a lot of practical homiletical ideas in this volume. This work is an exceptional classic reprint on the life of David. Here is a lifelike picture of the prophet-king and of his times. Devotional. See also, Frederick William Krummacher, **Elijah the Tishbite,** and his other work, **Elisha,** both by Zondervan Publishing House, n.d.

LANG, JOHN MARSHALL AND THOMAS KIRK. **Studies in the Book of Judges.** Minneapolis: Klock and Klock Christian Publishers, 1983.

One of the best treatments on the Book of Judges, giving accurate geographical and historical data and excellent biographical descriptions on the life of Samson. Devotional and exegetical.

EDERSHEIM, ALFRED. **Practical Truths from Elisha.** Grand Rapids: Kregel Publications, 1984.

A classic reprint giving a complete Scriptural account of the life and work of the prophet Elisha, featuring thorough research, solid exposition and spiritual applications.

MACDUFF, JOHN ROSS. **Elijah, The Prophet of Fire.** Minneapolis: Klock and Klock Christian Publishers, 1985.

In spite of their age, MacDuff's books are still eagerly sought after today. This classic reprint on the Life of Elijah is a must for ministers desiring to preach on this Bible character.

MEYER, FREDERICK BROTHERTON. **David: Shepherd, Psalmist, King.** London: Marshall, Morgan and Scott, 1953.

Meyer's devotional studies on the Life of David and his Psalms, are still sought after today. This author was simple and clear in his expositions on Bible characters. A rich devotional study.

————. **Elijah and the Secret of His Power.** London: Marshall, Morgan and Scott, 1954.

This work brings out the humanity of Elijah and demonstrates the secret of how God used him. Preachers will find this exposition and devotional study beneficial in preparing messages on the Life of Elijah.

————. **Samuel the Prophet.** London: Marshall, Morgan and Scott, 1902.

All of Meyers books on Bible characters are always practical and helpful. In this book, the life of Samuel is approached from a devotional exposition. Meyer draws practical applications from the life of Samuel.

PINK, ARTHUR WALKINGTON. **The Life of David.** 2 vols. Grand Rapids: Zondervan Publishing House, 1958.

Using First and Second Samuel, Pink develops the Life of David in a devotional and practical manner. These studies are rich in lessons about the struggling times that took place in the life of David. Calvinistic theology.

————. **The Life of Elijah.** England: The Banner of Truth Trust, 1963.

These excellent studies give an in-depth view of Elijah's ministry and apply it to the contemporary situation. This is a challenging study in the Book of Kings.

TAYLOR, WILLIAM MACKERGO. **David: King of Israel.** Grand Rapids: Baker Book House, 1961.

This is a classic reprint of 1886 on the life of David by an outstanding expository preacher. Taylor's exposition on David will help minister's prepare messages on this Bible character.

————. **Ruth the Gleaner, and Esther the Queen.** Grand Rapids: Baker Book House, 1961.

This is a reprint of an older volume first published in 1891. Any minister will benefit from Taylor's style of preaching on Bible characters. Since there are not a lot of good books on these two Bible characters, this work will be extremely beneficial.

REDPATH, ALAN. **The Making of a Man of God.** Westwood, N.J.: Fleming H. Revell Co., 1962.

A very helpful work on the life of David by an excellent preacher. These devotional studies will give the minister a lot of homiletical hints when preparing to preach on several aspects of David's life.

SCROGGIE, WILLIAM. **Joshua in the Light of the New Testament.** Grand Rapids: Kregel Publications, 1981.

In this older work, Scroggie shows the believers position in Christ and his walk with God as illustrated in the study of Joshua's life. An important reprint.

WISEMAN, LUKE H. **Practical Truths from Judges.** Grand Rapids: Kregel Publications, 1985.

A valuable classical reprint study that presents a general overview of the period of Judges along with an in-depth study of the lives of Barak, Gideon, Jephthah, and Samson. The author shows extensive research. Good commentaries on the Book of Judges are hard to find. Evangelical and Wesleyan in theology.

JOSHUA

BLAIKIE, WILLIAM GARDEN. **The Book of Joshua.** Minneapolis: Klock and Klock Christian Publishers, 1983.
This set is included in The Expositor's Bible. Blaikie devotes several chapters of this book to Joshua himself—his ancestry, character and succession. The remaining chapters contain a lengthy discussion rich in illustrations and applications useful to the Bible student and minister.

BUSH, GEORGE. **Notes Critical and Practical on Joshua and Judges.** Minneapolis: Klock and Klock Christian Publishers, 1981.
A valuable classic reprint that will enhance sermon preparation. Even though this work was published in 1852, it is still loaded with rich expository thoughts on the Books of Joshua and Judges.

PINK, ARTHUR A. **Gleanings in Joshua.** Chicago: Moody Press, 1981.
These studies in the life and times of Joshua were some of the last expositions to come from the gifted pen of this late author. Since Joshua is the capstone to the books of Moses and the foundation of those that follow, this work is extremely important and helpful to the minister. Calvinistic.

REDPATH, ALAN. **Victorious Christian Living.** Westwood, N.J.: Fleming H. Revell Co., 1955.
This devotional commentary gives practical insight into the Book of Joshua. While this work is not a verse-by-verse treatment, it will still serve as a homiletical guide to help the minister in preaching on this important Book of the Bible.

JUDGES

FAUSSET, ANDREW ROBERT. **A Critical and Expository Commentary on the Book of Judges.** Minneapolis: James and Klock Publishing Co., 1977.

This work has been hailed as the finest commentary on the Book of Judges. It is a classic reprint of an older edition. The author has given us a comprehensive and careful study on this Book of the Bible.

INRIG, GARY. **Hearts of Iron, Feet of Clay.** Chicago: Moody Press, 1979.

An extensive and recent exposition of this neglected Book of the Bible. The reader of this book will discover the great principles God reveals about His work in His people through this commentary on the Book of Judges.

WOOD, LEON JAMES. **Distressing Days of the Judges.** Grand Rapids: Zondervan Publishing House, 1975.

This work incorporates recent scholarship with practical application for daily living. A strongly conservative commentary on the Book of Judges. Wood gives a most satisfying exposition and perceptive study.

RODGERS, RICHARD. **Judges, A Facsimile of the 1615 Edition.** England: The Banner of Truth Trust, 1985.

This book is expensive, but it contains almost 1000 pages of excellent material on the Book of Judges. Though this work is quite old, it is still helpful for preaching material. This Puritan writer preached, in facsimile form, 103 sermons from the Book of Judges to his own congregation. Reformed.

RUTH

COX, SAMUEL AND THOMAS FULLER. **The Book of Ruth.** Minneapolis: Klock and Klock Christian Publishers, 1983.

This work contains two books in one volume. **The Book of Ruth** by Cox, and **Comment on Ruth** by Fuller. Both of these works are classic reprints. They reflect ripe scholarship and a strong devotional emphasis. At one time, it was difficult to obtain these books from any publisher. In addition, there is a small section called Notes on Jonah by Fuller.

HESLOP, WILLIAM G. **Rubies from Ruth.** Grand Rapids: Kregel Publications, 1982.

Heslop has written several excellent books on the Old Testament. This work is another in this series containing over 116 pages of Biblical truths from the Book of Ruth. See also, George G. Gardiner, **The Romance of Ruth,** Kregel Publications, 1977.

MCGEE, J. VERNON. **Ruth: The Romance of Redemption.** Nashville: Thomas Nelson Publishers, 1982.

J. Vernon McGee's examination of the Book of Ruth provides insight into redemption and love as they were codified by the law, then perfected by grace. This work is one of the best on the English text from a dispensational point of view. Evangelical. See also, Cyril J. Barber, **Ruth: An Expositional Commentary,** Moody Press, 1982.

TOURVILLE, ROBERT E. **A Devotional Commentary on The Book of Ruth.** New Wilmington, PA.: House of Bon Giovanni, 1984.

This work answers the question of why a Moabitess could be in the lineage of our Lord. The writer reveals the practical and devotional thoughts in the Book of Ruth. Pentecostal/Charismatic.

I AND II SAMUEL

BLACKWOOD, ANDREW WATTERSON. **Preaching from Samuel.** New York: Abingdon-Cokesbury Press, 1946.

Blackwood was an outstanding homiletics professor who wrote several books on preaching. This book is valuable for the minister wanting to preach or teach from the Books of Samuel. Evangelical.

BLAIKIE, WILLIAM G. **First Book of Samuel.** Minneapolis: Klock and Klock Christian Publishers, 1982.

This work was published in 1887–88 in The Expositor's Bible. Blaikie was an outstanding expositor on the Old Testament. If any minister wants to do some serious preaching on this Book of the Bible, he will want to consult Blaikie over and over again.

————. **Second Book of Samuel.** Minneapolis: Klock and Klock Christian Publishers, 1982.

This work was published in 1887–88 in the Expositor's Bible. Like the authors other works this one is a thorough and extremely practical exposition. A classic work.

CROCKETT, WILLIAM D. **A Harmony of Samuel, Kings, and Chronicles.** Grand Rapids: Baker Book House, 1985.

Just as a harmony of the Gospels is useful for tracing the life of Christ, this easy-to-use book provides the minister or Bible student with a reference guide to the history of the kings of Judah and Israel as preserved in the books of Samuel, Kings, and Chronicles.

DAVIS, JOHN JAMES. **The Birth of a Kingdom. Old Testament Studies.** Grand Rapids: Baker Book House, 1970.

A much needed work of recent scholarship. The author reveals the historical record of Samuel and Kings and highlights the biblical text with material from archaeological findings. Evangelical.

I AND II KINGS

FARRAR, F. W. **The First Book of Kings.** Minneapolis: Klock and Klock Christian Publishers, 1981.

Farrar was an excellent expositor of the Word of God. This work is included in The Expositor's Bible. It has now been reprinted as an individual commentary on the First Book of Kings. Watch out for some of his liberal tendencies.

————. **The Second Book of Kings.** Minneapolis: Klock and Klock Christian Publishers, 1981.

This book is included in The Expositor's Bible. The author writes on the same quality as he did in his sequal commentary on I Kings. Since it is difficult to find good commentaries on the Second Book of Kings, these expository studies will be of great value to the minister. Farrar is not always conservative in theology.

KIRK, THOMAS AND GEORGE RAWLINSON. **Studies in the Book of Kings.** Minneapolis: Klock and Klock Christian Publishers, 1983.

This work contains two books in one volume. **Solomon: His Life and His Works** by Kirk, 292 pages done in 1915, and **The Lives and Times of the Kings of Israel and Judah** by Rawlinson, 238 pages done in 1889. These classic works together provide a most readable and instructive resource covering the era following the death of David and concluding with the exile.

WHITCOMB, JOHN C., JR. **Solomon to the Exile: Studies in Kings and Chronicles.** Grand Rapids: Baker Book House, 1971.

Individual evangelical commentaries on the Books of Kings and Chronicles are scarce. This work by Whitcomb is brief but helpful in showing the cause of decline in Israel and Judah. Conservative. See also, Edwin R. Thiele, **The Mysterious Numbers of the Hebrew Kings,** Wm. B. Eerdmans Publishing Co., 1965.

I AND II CHRONICLES

BENNETT, WILLIAM HENRY. **An Exposition of Chronicles.** Minneapolis: Klock and Klock Christian Publishers, 1984.

In spite of the author's adherence to certain higher critical conclusions, what emerges in this work is a painstaking study which is at once understandable, generally reliable, and capable of providing rich insights into the Books of Chronicles.

MURPHY, JAMES GRACEY. **The Books of Chronicles.** Minneapolis: James and Klock Publishing Co., 1976.

This is one of the few individual commentaries on the Books of Chronicles. Murphy gives a concise treatment to these important books of the Bible. Reprint.

EZRA—NEHEMIAH

ADENEY, WALTER D. **Ezra and Nehemiah.** Minneapolis: Klock and Klock Christian Publishers, 1980.

The author gives careful examination of Israel's post-exilic history. Adeney was a British historian and theologian, expounding a most capable treatment of the Books of Ezra and Nehemiah, which readers of the English text will enjoy.

IRONSIDE, HENRY ALLAN. **Ezra, Nehemiah and Esther.** New Jersey: Loizeaux Brothers, 1979.

A reprint from an author who gets to the heart of any Scripture in a clear manner. These three closely-linked books, covering the period of Jewish history following the captivity, illustrate the various responses man can make to the commands of God. Devotional.

REDPATH, ALAN. **Victorious Christian Service.** Westwood, N.J.: Fleming H. Revell Co., 1958.

Redpath is an outstanding Bible expositor, who has gone to the Book of Nehemiah to find for himself and all other Christians the principles of Christian service. This work gives the minister some strong homiletical hints for preaching on Nehemiah.

SWINDOLL, CHARLES ROZELL. **Hand Me Another Brick.** Nahsville: Thomas Nelson, 1978.

This book is loaded with homiletical ideas on Nehemiah. Swindoll's clear exposition, his marked emphasis upon the gospel's practical applications, and his personable style have catapulted him into public demand as a preacher and teacher. An excellent presentation of the principles of leadership, and how to motivate oneself and others. See also, Cyril J. Barber, **Nehemiah and the Dynamics of Leadership,** Loizeaux Brothers, 1976.

ESTHER

MCGEE, JOHN VERNON. **Esther: The Romance of Redemption.** Nashville: Thomas Nelson Publishers, 1982.

This informal historical analysis reveals an appealing new dimension of the Book of Esther as it becomes apparent that God in His providence is guiding our lives today just as He did then. Devotional and Evangelical.

RALEIGH, ALEXANDER. **Book of Esther: Its Practical Lessons and Dramatic Scenes.** Minneapolis: Klock and Klock Christian Publishers, 1980.

Recreates the life and times of Hadassah, the Jewish girl, who became Esther the Queen and wife of Ahasuerus. This excellent commentary on the Book of Esther will be a valuable edition to any minister's library. Devotional.

THE POETICAL BOOKS

BULLOCK, C. HASSEL. **Introduction to Old Testament Poetic Books.** Chicago: Moody Press, 1984.

In this volume, Bullock shares the motivation and compulsion of the wisdom teachers. This work contains extensive indexing for a detailed study of the Poetical Books. Evangelical.

JOB

BLACKWOOD, ANDREW WATTERSON, JR. **A Devotional Introduction to Job.** Grand Rapids: Baker Book House, 1970.

This commentary will serve best as a homiletical guide to the book of Job. In addition, Blackwood gives some excellent devotional insights into this Old Testament Book.

CARYL, JOSEPH. **An Exposition of Job.** Grand Rapids: Kregel Publications, reprint.

This Puritan work originally appeared in twelve volumes and was published between 1644 and 1666. Since then, the work has been abridged and can be a valuable edition to any minister's library.

CHAPPELL, CLOVIS G. **Sermons From Job.** Nashville: Abingdon Press, 1957.

A practical, lucid, and reverent treatment of one of the most profound books of the Old Testament. Chappell's books of sermons are extremely helpful to ministers. Here is another work from the pen of a great evangelical Methodist preacher.

GIBSON, EDGAR CHARLES SUMMER. **The Book of Job.** Minneapolis: Klock and Klock Christian Publishers, 1978.

Not only is this commentary rich in word studies, but the author's outline is also very thorough, giving one an immediate familiarity with Job. This exposition was first published in 1899.

GREEN, WILLIAM H. **The Argument of the Book of Job Unfolded.** Minneapolis: Klock and Klock Christian Publishers, 1980.

A recent reprint of a real classic on the central ideas of the Book of Job. This book continues to be in demand in spite of its age. Green shows that Job was triumphant over Satan.

MORGAN, G. CAMPBELL. **Answers of Jesus to Job.** Grand Rapids: Baker Book House, 1964.

Morgan has some outstanding expositions of the Bible. In this work the author shows how Jesus Christ answers many of the questions raised in the Book of Job. A practical exposition. For more homiletical helps, see also, David Thomas, **Book of Job,** Kregel Publications, 1981.

PSALMS

ALEXANDER, JOSEPH ADDISON. **The Psalms Translated and Explained.** Grand Rapids: Zondervan Publishing House, reprint.

Here is a valuable classic on the Book of Psalms first published in 1864. This work is a soundly, scholarly and warmly evangelical commentary on the vast teaching of the Psalms.

BONAR, ANDREW ALEXANDER. **Christ and His Church**

in the Book of Psalms. Grand Rapids: Kregel Publications, 1978.

This commentary is written very simply, expressively, and precisely. It comes to grips with everyday life. Bonar richly unfolds the excitement, rejoicing, sorrowing, agonizing-more nearly every human emotion. Devotional.

BRIDGES, CHARLES. **Commentary on Psalm 119.** London: The Banner of Truth Trust, 1979.

Bridges commentary on this Psalm is outstanding. This Puritan author is known for his work on Proverbs. If you are going to preach on this Psalm, Bridges will give you a great deal of devotional help.

CHAPPELL, CLOVIS G. **Sermons From the Psalms.** New York: Abingdon-Cokesbury Press, 1931.

Here is a stimulating treatment of a select number of Psalms from a gifted writer. Chappell applies the messages of these Psalms to modern times. The minister will find excellent sermon material in this work.

CLARKE, ARTHUR G. **Analytical Studies in the Psalms.** Grand Rapids: Kregel Publications, 1979.

An excellent treatment of the Book of Psalms, featuring homiletical outlines, and practical applications. This classic study on the Psalms presents an analysis of each Psalm and its relationship in the Canon of Scripture.

COX, SAMUEL. **The Pilgrim Psalms: An Exposition of the Songs of Degrees.** Minneapolis: Klock and Klock Christian Publishers, 1982.

An excellent series of expository studies covering Psalm 120–134. It is probably some of the best expositions on these Psalms to be found anywhere in print. Cox was an outstanding expository preacher.

DAVIS, JOHN JAMES. **The Perfect Shepherd: Studies in the Twenty-Third Psalm.** Winona Lake, IN: Brethren Missionary Herald Books, 1979.

The same quality is exemplified in this work as is found in the author's other writings. This is a complete treatment of this popular Psalm. See also, Haddon W. Robinson, **Psalm Twenty-Three,** Moody Press, 1968.

LEUPOLD, HERBERT CARL. **Exposition of the Psalms.** Minneapolis: Wartburg Press, 1959. Reprint. Grand Rapids: Baker Book House, 1969.

This standard work was written by an evangelical Lutheran Old Testament scholar. It contains over 1000 pages of expository material on the Book of Psalms. A valuable study.

LLOYD-JONES, DAVID MARTYN. **Faith on Trial,** Grand Rapids: Wm. B. Erdmans Publishing Co., 1965.

This is a series of expository meditations on the well-known Psalm 73. Such problems are dealt with as David's self-abasement, the theme of nearness to God, why God allows the unrighteous to prosper, the problem of suffering and others.

MACLAREN, ALEXANDER. **The Psalms.** 3 vols. Minneapolis: Klock and Klock Christian Publishers, 1981.

Maclaren did his best work in these three volumes on The Psalms. These volumes are also included in The Expositor's Bible. Practical and expository studies.

MEYER, FREDERICK BROTHERTON. **The Shepherd Psalm.** Fort Washington, PA.: Christian Literature Crusade, 1953.

Meyer has put together a warmly devotional exposition on Psalm Twenty-Three. This work will aid the minister that attempts to do a series of messages on this important Psalm of the Old Testament. See also, W. Philip Keller, **A Shepherd Looks At Psalm 23,** Baker Book House, 1979.

PEROWNE, JOHN JAMES STEWART. **The Book of Psalms.** 2 vols. Grand Rapids: Zondervan Publishing House, 1966.

This classic work was originally published in 1878. Perowne provides a complete background on each Psalm and clear-cut concise marginal notes that give the reader "at-a-glance" information. Reformed. See also, David Dickson, **A Commentary on the Psalms,** 2 vols., Klock and Klock Christian Publishers, 1980.

SPURGEON, CHARLES HADDON. **The Treasury of David: A Commentary on the Psalms.** 3 vols. Peabody, MA: Hendrickson Publishers, 1985.

Rich devotional material that will prove invaluable in the

minister's personal life and a great source of material for teaching and preaching. More than a commentary, this great work includes a theological collection, a collection of illustrative extracts from the whole range of literature and a series of homiletical hints on almost every verse in Psalms. He drew from over a thousand authors and sources, classical, Jewish, and Christian from all periods of church history.

PROVERBS

ARNOT, WILLIAM. **Studies in Proverbs.** Grand Rapids: Kregel Publications, 1980.

Arnot's thoughts on selected texts in the Book of Proverbs offer practical instruction and spiritual direction for a Christ-centered life. The author's aim was to be doctrinal, spiritual and practical. A classic work. See also, James R. Draper, Jr., **Proverbs: The Secret of Beautiful Living,** Tyndale House Publishers, 1981.

BRIDGES, CHARLES. **Proverbs.** London: The Banner of Truth Trust, 1959.

Bridges was a famous Puritan writer. This work will provide a minister with lots of Biblical direction and spiritual insight into the Book of Proverbs. Although this book was first published in 1846, it is still considered a valuable classic.

IRONSIDE, HENRY ALLEN. **Notes on the Book of Proverbs.** New York: Loizeaux Brothers, n.d.

While this work is not detailed or profound, it will still help the minister to find illustrative material on the Book of Proverbs. Ironside was known for his keen studies and expositions on many subjects and Books of the Bible.

LAWSON, GEORGE. **Proverbs.** Grand Rapids: Kregel Publications, 1980.

Lawson is well known for his **Lectures on the History of Joseph** and his **Discourses on Esther, Ruth and David.** This practical classic on Proverbs will bring a source of spiritual strength, wisdom and direction for every minister and Bible student of the Word of God. Devotional.

WARDLAW, RALPH. **Books of Proverbs.** 3 vols. Minneapolis: Klock and Klock Christian Publishers, 1982.

Wardlaw was a well-known evangelical Scottish preacher in his day. He was committed to upholding the Truth of the Word in his expository and theological studies. This massive classic work of expositions will be of great value for any minister preparing a series of messages from the Book of Proverbs. For another homiletical study, see also, David Thomas, **Book of Proverbs,** Kregel Publications, 1982.

ECCLESIASTES

COX, SAMUEL. **The Book of Ecclesiastes. The Expositor's Bible.** 6 vols. Grand Rapids: Baker Book House, reprint.

Cox continues his valuable expository style in this classic work on the Book of Ecclesiastes. These expositions will give new insight into this neglected Book of the Bible.

HENGSTENBERG, ERNEST W. **Commentary on Ecclesiastes.** Translated by D. W. Simon. Grand Rapids: Kregel Publications, reprint.

This work is both scholarly and practical in its approach to the Book of Ecclesiastes. It is a classic reprint of an older edition that is thorough and conservative in theology. Devotional.

LEUPOLD, HERBERT CARL. **Expositions of Ecclesiastes.** Grand Rapids: Baker Book House, 1966.

Although Leupold rejects Solomonic authorship, his commentary is still one of the best in print. This work is based on a careful study of the original text with many practical applications to everyday life. Conservative. See also, Walter C. Kaiser, JR., **Ecclesiastes: Total Life,** Moody Press, n.d.

MACDONALD, JAMES MADISON. **The Book of Ecclesiastes.** Minneapolis: Klock and Klock Christian Publishers, 1981.

This classic work was first published in 1856. MacDonald does not slight the demands of scholarship, but in a clear, readable way draws out and then applies the teaching of the Book of Ecclesiastes. Very helpful.

SWINDOLL, CHARLES R. **Living on the Ragged Edge.** Waco, Texas: Word Books Publishers, 1985.

If you are looking for preaching material on the Book of Ecclesiastes, Swindoll is a must. The author offers many fresh insights into Solomon's life through this expositional commentary. Evangelical.

WARDLAW, RALPH. **An Exposition of Ecclesiastes.** Minneapolis: Klock and Klock Christian Publishers, 1981.

Much sought after, this commentary has been a source of valuable information ever since it was published in 1821. It is a series of excellent expository sermons on the Book of Ecclesiastes. Wardlaw is always stimulating and knows how to apply the text to the heart and mind of his readers.

SONG OF SOLOMON

BERNARD OF CLAIRVAUX. **The Song of Solomon.** Minneapolis: Klock and Klock Christian Publishers, 1982.

Bernard of Clairvaux was an outstanding writer of some of our most enduring hymns of the Church. This classical devotional commentary, formerly titled **Cantice Canticorum** has now been translated into English. Bernard takes the view that the Song of Solomon lays bare the vital union between Christ and the believer.

DURHAM, JAMES. **An Exposition of the Song of Solomon.** Minneapolis: Klock and Klock Christian Publishers, 1983.

Durham understands the Song of Solomon as an allegory of the relationship between Christ and the believer. This classic devotional study was first published in 1668 and contains over 460 pages of practical material. See also, John Gill, **An Exposition of the Book of Solomon's Song,** Sovereign Grace Publishers, 1970.

IRONSIDE, HENRY ALLAN. **The Song of Solomon.** Neptune, N.J.: Loizeaux Brothers, 1970.

Ironside approaches The Song of Solomon from an allegorical and typological point of view. This devotional study will give the minister some good preaching material.

NEE, WATCHMAN. **Song of Songs.** Translated by Elizabeth K. Mei and Daniel Smith. Fort Washington, Penn.: Christian Literature Crusade, 1965.

The burden to present this commentary arose in the translator, Daniel Smith, because of the rich value The Song of Solomon has in its typological interpretation. A practical study.

TAYLOR, JAMES HUDSON. **Union and Communion.** Chicago: Moody Press, n.d.

In this work, Taylor has produced an excellent practical and devotional study on The Song of Solomon. This allegorical work was first published in 1893.

PROPHETIC BOOKS
THE PROPHETS

CHAPPELL, CLOVIS G. **And The Prophets.** New York: Abingdon Press, 1956.

Chappell presents a practical study of the personality, characteristics, experiences, and messages of The Prophets. He applies their messages to the needs of today. This work contains a lot of helpful preaching material. For other preaching values, see also, Andrew W. Blackwood, **Preaching from Prophetic Books,** Abingdon Press, 1946, and Kyle M. Yates, **Preaching from the Prophets,** Broadman Press, 1942.

ELLISON, HENRY LEOPOLD. **Men Spoke from God: Studies in the Hebrew Prophets.** Grand Rapids: Wm. B. Eerdmans Publishing Co., 1958.

Ellison gives a complete look at the ancient spokesman of God, their books, and the key to comprehension of their message by the modern reader. You will not want to accept some of his interpretations. See also, Henry L. Ellison, **The Prophets of Israel,** Wm. B. Eerdmans Publishing Co., 1969.

WOOD, LEON J. **The Prophets of Israel.** Grand Rapids: Baker Book House, 1979.

This is a helpful study of the writing and nonwriting

prophets. Wood studies the prophets as people, in the day and circumstances in which they lived, making their messages more understandable.

YOUNG, EDWARD JOSEPH. **My Servants, the Prophets.** Grand Rapids: Wm. B. Eerdmans Publishing Co., 1952.

Young has written one of the best works on the prophetic institution. This work develops the prophetic message and ministry from a conservative viewpoint. See also, Sanford C. Yoder, **He Gave Some Prophets: The Old Testament Prophets and Their Message,** Herald Press, 1964.

MAJOR PROPHETS
ISAIAH

ALEXANDER, JOSEPH ADDINSON. **Commentary on the Prophecies of Isaiah.** Minneapolis: Klock and Klock Christian Publishers, 1981.

Alexander's classic work on Isaiah was first published in 1846. His new edition of 1861 was designed for the English reader. This conservative work is a verse-by-verse treatment of the Hebrew text. Amillennial.

ALLIS, OSWALD THOMPSON. **The Unity of Isaiah: A Study in Prophecy.** Philadelphia: Presbyterian and Reformed Publishing Co., 1950.

This work refutes the liberal view of the Deutero-Isaiah theory. It is one of the best books on this important study about the Book of Isaiah. See also, Edward J. Young, **Who Wrote Isaiah?,** Wm. B. Eerdmans Publishing Co., 1958.

CRISWELL, WALLIE AMOS. **Isaiah: An Exposition.** Grand Rapids: Zondervan Publishing House, 1979.

Criswell brings forth a dynamic, expository, exposition of the Book of Isaiah. This work has some excellent preaching material. Conservative.

CULVER, ROBERT DUNCAN. **The Sufferings and Glory of the Lord's Righteous Servant.** Moline, IL.: Christian Service Foundation, 1958.

This work contains an exposition of Isaiah 52:13–53:12.

Culver handles these important verses in Isaiah with great skill. Conservative. See also, John Brown, **The Sufferings and Glories of the Messiah,** Sovereign Grace Publishers, 1959, and David Baron, **The Servant of Jehovah,** Zondervan Publishing House, 1954.

JENNINGS, FREDERICK CHARLES. **Studies in Isaiah.** Neptune, N.J.: Loizeaux Brothers, 1966.

Even though this work was first published in 1935, it still has great devotional value in the study of Isaiah. Jennings was a Plymouth Brethren writer. Conservative.

KELLY, WILLIAM. **An Exposition of the Book of Isaiah.** 4th. ed. Minneapolis: Klock and Klock Christian Publishers, 1979.

This classic exposition by Kelly was first published in 1896. He defends the unity of Isaiah with sound conservative scholarship. Premillennial.

LEUPOLD, HERBERT CARL. **An Exposition of Isaiah.** 2 vols. Grand Rapids: Baker Book House, 1968–71.

Leupold ably defends the unity of Isaiah. He gives a helpful understanding of the Hebrew text for the English reader. This is a serious study of the Book of Isaiah. Amillennial.

MEYER, FREDERICK BROTHERTON. **Christ in Isaiah.** Fort Washington, Penn.: Christian Literature Crusade, 1970.

This is an outstanding devotional commentary on Isaiah 40–55. Meyer writes with freshness, simplicity and profound insight into these Messianic chapters. See also, Allan A. MacRae, **The Gospel of Isaiah,** Moody Press, 1977.

MORGAN, GEORGE CAMPBELL. **The Prophecy of Isaiah.** Analyzed Bible. 2 vols. Grand Rapids: Baker Book House, 1971.

If you are looking for a good analysis of the Book of Isaiah, this work by Morgan is a must. He gives a minister a lot of homiletical helps in this book. See also, William E. Vine, **Isaiah: Prophecies, Promises, Warning.** Zondervan Publishing House, 1968.

YOUNG, EDWARD JOSEPH. **The Book of Isaiah.** New International Commentary on the Old Testament. 3 vols. Grand Rapids: Wm. B. Eerdmans Publishing Co., 1965–72.

Young has written the most important evangelical commentary on the Book of Isaiah for years to come! This work is thorough, and provides the kind of exegetical studies that good preachers and teachers need. You will not agree with his Amillennial approach to Isaiah, but these 1700 pages are worth the money. See also, Edward J. Young, **Isaiah 53: A Devotional and Expository Study,** Wm. B. Eerdmans Publishing Co., 1952.

JEREMIAH AND LAMENTATIONS

FEINBERG, CHARLES LEE. **Jeremiah.** A Commentary. Grand Rapids: Zondervan Publishing House, 1982.
Feinburg includes a good introduction to the Book of Jeremiah that explains the book's historical background, the life of Jeremiah, the theology of his prophecies, and outline of the book and a good bibliography. This work gives a detailed verse-by-verse explanation of the text. Premillennial.
LAETSCH, THEODORE FERDINAND KARL. **Bible Commentary: Jeremiah.** St. Louis: Concordia Publishing House, 1952.
In addition to providing a storehouse of exegetical information on the Book of Jeremiah, Laetsch also includes an excellent commentary on the Book of Lamentations.
MORGAN, GEORGE CAMPBELL. **Studies in the Prophecy of Jeremiah.** London: Oliphants Press, 1963.
Morgan analyzes the character of this prophet and shows a minister how to expound on these two books of the Bible. Amillennial. See also, Frederick B. Meyer, **Jeremiah: Priest and Prophet,** Christian Literature Crusade, 1970.
ORELLI, HANS CONRAD VON. **The Prophecies of Jeremiah.** Minneapolis: Klock and Klock Christian Publishers, 1977.
This classic work is a verse-by-verse treatment preceded by an enlightening introduction which covers Jeremiah's name, descent, time, personal characteristics, form of prophecy, and the background of the book. Conservative and expository.
THOMPSON, JOHN ARTHUR. **The Book of Jeremiah.**

New International Commentary on the Old Testament. Grand
Rapids: Wm. B. Eerdmans Publishing Co., 1980.

Thompson has made an important contribution to the study
of the Book of Jeremiah. This detailed, up-to-date commentary
is evangelical in Theology.

EZEKIEL

BLACKWOOD, ANDREW W., JR. **Ezekiel, Prophecy of
Hope.** Grand Rapids: Baker Book House, 1965.

Even though Blackwood takes the Amillennial approach to
the Book of Ezekiel, this work still has practical homiletical
value for ministers.

FAIRBAIRN, PATRICK. **An Exposition of Ezekiel.** Minneapolis: Klock and Klock Christian Publishers, 1979.

In this valuable expository study, Fairbairn ably handles
some difficult passages of Scripture from the book of Ezekiel.
This classic work was first published in 1851. Amillennial. See
also, Ernst Wilhelm Hengstenberg, **The Prophecies of the
Prophet Ezekiel,** James and Klock Publishing Co., 1976.

FEINBURG, CHARLES LEE. **The Prophecy of Ezekiel.**
Chicago: Moody Press, 1969.

Dr. Feinburg is a conservative Old Testament writer. This
work is a chapter by chapter study on the neglected Book of
Ezekiel. Premillennial. See also, WM. G. Heslop, **Pearls from
the Prophet Ezekiel,** Kregel Publications, 1976.

DANIEL

CRISWELL, WALLIS AMOS. **Expository Sermons on the
Book of Daniel.** Grand Rapids: Zondervan Publishing House,
1974.

Criswell gives an excellent analysis of Daniel and its applica-
ble truths. These expository sermons are filled with word studies, background information and colorful descriptions. Premillennial and evangelical.

LEUPOLD, HERBERT CARL. **Exposition of Daniel.** Minneapolis: Augsburg Publishing Co., 1961.

This conservative work is helpful for exegetical value. Even though Leupold approaches the Book of Daniel from an Amillennial point of view, this volume is still worth consulting. See also, Edward J. Young, **The Prophecy of Daniel: A Commentary,** Wm. B. Eerdmans Publishing Co., 1949.

MCCLAIN, ALVA J. **Daniel's Prophecy of the Seventy Weeks.** 7th ed. Grand Rapids: Zondervan Publishing House, 1940.

This is an extremely helpful exposition of Daniel 9:24–27. Even though this work is brief, it will be a valuable contribution on Daniel. Premillennial. See also, Frederick A. Tatford, **Daniel and His Prophecy,** Klock and Klock Christian Publishers, 1980.

PUSEY, EDWARD BOUVERIE. **Daniel the Prophet.** Minneapolis: Klock and Klock Christian Publishers, 1978.

This is a classic conservative work that was first published in 1885. These nine lectures on the Book of Daniel were first given at Oxford University to combat skepticism then sweeping the theological world. Amillennial.

STRAUSS, LEHMAN. **The Prophecies of Daniel.** Neptune, N.J.: Loizeaux Brothers, 1969.

If a minister wants to preach a series of messages from the Book of Daniel, he will want to consult Strauss. This work is thoroughly conservative and premillennial in its viewpoint. See also, Charles Boutiflower, **In and Around the Book of Daniel,** Zondervan Publishing House, 1963.

WALVOORD, JOHN FLIPSE, **Daniel: The Key to Prophetic Revelation.** Chicago: Moody Press, 1971.

This work is a detailed, systematic analysis of the book of Daniel with emphasis on studying and refuting nonbiblical views. Premillennial and conservative. See also, John C. Whitcomb, Jr., **Darius the Mede: A Study in Historical Identification,** Wm. B. Eerdmans Publishing Co., 1959.

WRIGHT, CHARLES. H. **Studies in Daniel's Prophecy.** Minneapolis: Klock and Klock Christian Publishers, 1980.

Wright was an outstanding writer on the Old Testament.

This classic work places special emphasis on the historical aspects of the Book of Daniel. Amillennial and conservative.

MINOR PROPHETS

FEINBURG, CHARLES LEE. **The Minor Prophets.** Chicago: Moody Press, 1976.
Feinburg has written an excellent comprehensive commentary on all twelve of the minor prophets. This work is free of footnotes, and devotional in style. It was formerly published under the title, **Major Messages on the Minor Prophets.** Premillennial. See also, Henry A. Ironside, **Notes on the Minor Prophets,** Loizeaux Brothers, 1909.

GAEBELEIN, FRANK ELY. **Four Minor Prophets.** Chicago: Moody Press, 1970.
In this work, the author gives a conservative devotional study on Obadiah, Jonah, Habakkuk, and Haggai. Gaebelein makes these important books come alive. Premillennial.

LAETSCH, THEODORE FERDINAND KARL. **The Minor Prophets.** St. Louis: Concordia Publishing House, 1956.
Laetsch regards the biblical text of the Minor Prophets to be trustworthy and reliable. This is a historical and devotional study. Amillennial and conservative.

MORGAN, GEORGE CAMPBELL. **The Minor Prophets: The Men and Their Messages.** Westwood, N.J.: Fleming H. Revell Co., 1960.
In these brief studies, Morgan finds the theme of the twelve minor prophets to be about God's love. Many feel that Morgan did his best work on these important Prophets of the Old Testament. Conservative.

ORELLI, CONRAD VON. **The Twelve Minor Prophets.** Minneapolis: Klock and Klock Christian Publishers, 1981.
The meanings of Hebrew words are brought to light by a simple but full English explanation. This classic work is based upon sound scholarship. Conservative.

PUSEY, EDWARD BOUVERIE. **The Minor Prophets: A**

Commentary, Explanatory and Practical. 2 vols. Grand Rapids: Baker Book House, 1967.

In spite of its age, this classic set is still in great demand today. Ministers will find homiletical material, historical information and many practical applications in these important studies of the minor prophets. Amillennial.

TATFORD, FREDERICK A. **The Minor Prophets.** 3 vols. Minneapolis: Klock and Klock Christian Publishers, 1981.

Tatford was a specialist on the minor prophets. These expository studies are well-researched and show a judicious conservative exposition. Premillennial. For homiletical ideas, see also, James Montgomery Boice, **The Minor Prophets,** Zondervan Publishing House, 1985.

HONEYCUTT, ROY L. **Hosea and His Message.** Nashville: Broadman Press, 1979.

This brief exposition focuses on the basic theme and corollary ideas in the experience and teaching of the prophet Hosea. Conservative.

MAYS, JAMES LUTHER. **Hosea, A Commentary.** Old Testament Library. Philadelphia: Westminster Press, 1969.

Unfortunately, many works in this series contain liberal theology. This critical study of the book of Hosea by Luther, will aid the minister in the study of the original text.

MORGAN, GEORGE CAMPBELL. **Hosea: the Heart and Holiness of God.** Grand Rapids: Baker Book House, 1974.

Morgan's expository study on the Book of Hosea is probably his best work. This excellent exposition shows how this Hebrew Prophet and his teaching foreshadowed the message of the Savior and the Epistles of Paul. Amillennial.

JOEL

ALLEN, LESLIE C. **The Books of Joel, Obadiah, Jonah and Micah.** New International Commentary on the Old Testament. Grand Rapids: Wm. B. Eerdmans Publishing Co., 1976.

This work contains some valuable introductions, special

notes, complete expositions, and footnotes prepared by lead-ing conservative scholars.

AMOS

CRIPPS, RICHARD STAFFORD. **A Commentary on the Book of Amos.** Minneapolis: Klock and Klock Christian Pub-lishers, 1981.
Even though this book was published in 1929, it was revised in 1955. This full exposition contains many practical applica-tions to the needs of today. Conservative.
HOWARD, JAMES KEIR. **Amos Among the Prophets.** Grand Rapids: Baker Book House, 1967.
This well-balanced commentary on the Book of Amos will be a valuable edition to a minister's library. It is conservative, practical, and historical in its approach to this minor prophet.
MAYS, JAMES LUTHER. **Amos: A Commentary.** Old Testament Library. Philadelphia: Westminster Press, 1969.
Mays gives the reader a lot of background information on the Book of Amos. This is a helpful verse-by-verse commentary.

OBADIAH

MARBURY, EDWARD. **Obadiah and Habakkuk.** Minne-apolis: Klock and Klock Christian Publishers, 1981.
Dr. Marbury's work on Obadiah and Habakkuk is a true classic. Good studies on these two books of the Bible are rare. This work will be of great benefit to every minister and Bible student.

JONAH

BANKS, WILLIAM L. **Jonah: The Reluctant Prophet.** Chi-cago: Moody Press, 1966.
In this work, Banks gives the reader an up-to-date exposi-

tion of the Book of Jonah. This commentary will aid the minister in devotional thoughts, historical background and word studies from this important Hebrew prophet.

BURN, SAMUEL CLIFT. **The Prophet Jonah.** Minneapolis: Klock and Klock Christian Publishers, 1981.

Burns delivered these expository messages to a congregation in England several years ago. Every minister will be able to glean some homiletical treasures from this practical work.

EXELL, JOSEPH S. **Practical Truths from Jonah.** Grand Rapids: Kregel Publications, 1982.

This verse-by-verse exposition deals with the practical aspects of the Book of Jonah. Exell was an excellent devotional writer. Conservative.

KIRK, THOMAS. **Jonah: His Life and Mission.** Minneapolis: Klock and Klock Christian Publishers, 1981.

These lectures on the Book of Jonah are expository, fresh, and suggestive. Kirk has an intriging way of making Bible characters come alive. Conservative.

MARTIN, HUGH. **The Prophet Jonah: His Character and Mission to Nineveh.** London: Banner of Truth Trust, 1958.

This Scottish preacher wrote one of the best devotional works on Jonah. This classic work is loaded with spiritual insight and application.

MICAH

BENNETT, T. MILES. **The Book of Micah.** Grand Rapids: Baker Book House, 1968.

This is a practical book that will aid the minister in preparing a series of messages on the Book of Micah.

NAHUM

MAIER, WALTER A. **The Book of Nahum.** St. Louis: Concordia Publishing House, 1959.

Maier has written the best commentary on the Book of Nahum. This valuable work will be of great help to the expositor. Conservative.

HABAKKUK

LLOYD-JONES, DAVID MARTYN. **From Fear To Faith.** London: Inter-Varsity Fellowship, 1964.
These practical, expository messages on the Book of Habakkuk will enhance any preachers library. See also, Marbury's commentary, **Obadiah and Habakkuk.**

ZEPHANIAH

TATFORD, FREDERICK A. **Prophet of Royal Blood.** Eastbourne, Sussex, Eng.: Prophetic Witness Publishing House, 1973.
This work is one of a series on the Minor Prophets by Tatford. See also, comments on Tatford under "Minor Prophets."

HAGGAI

MOORE, THOMAS V. **A Commentary on Haggai, Malachi and Zechariah.** London: Banner of Truth Trust, 1960.
Moore's devotional commentary on Haggai, Malachi and Zechariah will be a valuable addition to the minister's library. Evangelical.

ZECHARIAH

BARON, DAVID. **The Visions and Prophecies of Zechariah.** Grand Rapids: Kregel Publications, 1962.
This work is one of the best commentaries on the Book of Zechariah. Even though this book was first published in 1918, it still contains valuable information on the messianic prophecies contained in Zechariah.

LEUPOLD, HERBERT CARL. **Exposition of Zechariah.** Grand Rapids: Baker Book House, 1970.

Dr. Leupold furnishes the minister with a helpful introduction discussing authorship, date, and purposes, and helpful comments on the prophetic predictions of the book of Zechariah. Amillennial.

MEYER, FREDERICK BROTHERTON. **The Prophet of Hope: Studies in Zechariah.** London: Marshall, Morgan and Scott, 1952.

This devotional commentary on the Book of Zechariah gives many practical lessons and applications for today. Premillennial.

UNGER, MERRILL FREDERICK. **Zechariah: Prophet of Messiah's Glory.** Grand Rapids: Zondervan Publishing House, 1963.

Dr. Unger has contributed a major work on the Book of Zechariah. This valuable commentary is based upon the original text. The author has brought to bear all the latest archaeological knowledge and findings that contribute to the subject of this book of prophecy. Premillennial.

WRIGHT, CHARLES HENRY HAMILTON. **Zechariah and His Prophecies, Considered in Relation to Modern Criticism.** Minneapolis: Klock and Klock Christian Publishers, 1980.

This massive commentary of 694 pages was first published in 1879. The work was edited by the renowned Dr. Franz Delitzsch. Dr. Wright's exposition is both scholarly and conservative. Amillennial.

MALACHI

MORGAN, GEORGE CAMPBELL. **Malachi's Message for Today.** Grand Rapids: Baker Book House, 1972.

Although Morgan's work on Malachi is not extensive, it is an extremely valuable and practical commentary. It was first published in 1898 under the title, **Wherein Have We Robbed God?**

BOOKS ON THE NEW TESTAMENT
NEW TESTAMENT BIBLE INTRODUCTIONS

HARRISON, EVERETT FALCONER. **Introduction to the New Testament.** Grand Rapids: Wm. B. Eerdmans Publishing Co., 1964.

This work is highly acclaimed as one of the best New Testament Introductions today. For another oustanding work, see also, Donald Guthrie, **New Testament Introduction,** Inter-Varsity, 1981.

TENNEY, MERRILL CHAPIN. **New Testament Survey.** Grand Rapids: Wm. B. Eerdmans Publishing Co., 1961.

Tenney is a highly respected authority on the New Testament. This historical and analytical work is a revision of the author's earlier work published in 1953. It is still used as a textbook in many colleges and seminaries.

————. **New Testament Times.** Grand Rapids: Wm. B. Eerdmans Publishing Co., 1965.

For a well illustrated and written cultural background on the New Testament, Tenney is extremely helpful. This work puts New Testament people and events into their proper historical setting.

NEW TESTAMENT THEOLOGY

BERNARD, THOMAS DEHANY. **The Progress of Doctrine in the New Testament.** Minneapolis: Klock and Klock Christian Publishers, 1979.

These lectures present the idea that doctrine in the New Testament has developed in the order of their canonical arrangement. This series of lectures survey the entire field of New Testament theology. A classic reprint.

GUTHRIE, DONALD. **New Testament Theology.** Downers Grove, IL: Inter-Varsity, 1981.

There are a lot of books on New Testament Theology, but there are very few good conservative works. Guthrie is a welcome addition to this field of study. Conservative. For an older evangelical work, see also, Charles Caldwell Ryrie, **Biblical Theology of the New Testament,** Moody Press, 1959.

LADD, GEORGE ELDON. **A Theology of the New Testament.** Grand Rapids: Wm. B. Eerdmans Publishing Co., 1974.

Ladd's work of mature scholarship is rapidly becoming the standard text on New Testament Theology. This is a welcome conservative alternative to Bultmann and other liberal theologians. For an Arminian approach, see also, Chester K. Lehman, **Biblical Theology of the New Testament,** Herald Press, 1981.

NEW TESTAMENT WORD STUDIES

The New International Dictionary of the New Testament Theology. 3 vols. Edited by COLIN BROWN. Grand Rapids: Zondervan Publishing House, 1975.

This set is a treasure house of knowledge for the study of Greek words. A knowledge of the Greek language is not a requirement for using this set. All pastor's will want to purchase these valuable word studies. See also, **Scripture Index to the New International Dictionary of New Testament Theology** by the same publisher.

Theological Dictionary of the New Testament. Edited by GEOFFREY W. BROMILEY. Grand Rapids: Wm. B. Eerdmans Publishing Co., 1985.

This handy dictionary is an abridgement of the ten-volume edition of Kittel. With this one volume, the non-technical reader can have many valuable insights into the meanings of the words of the Greek New Testament.

EARLE, RALPH. **Word Meanings in the New Testament.** 6 vols. Kansas City, MO.: Beacon Hill Press, 1977.

Earle deals with the meaning of interesting and significant words in the New Testament. Pastors and teachers need to give close attention to the meaning of words. Arminian/Wesleyan.

The Complete Biblical Library. 16 vols. Edited by RALPH HARRIS. Springfield, MO: Gospel Publishing House, 1986.

This set will enrich the personal study of the New Testament for any minister or student. It's a Study Bible, a Greek/English Dictionary, and a Harmony of the Gospels. It is written by more than 300 evangelical and Pentecostal scholars. The English version is to be completed in 1988.

ROBERTSON, ARCHIBALD THOMAS. **Word Pictures in the New Testament.** 6 vols. Nashville: Broadman Press, 1930–33.

These word studies can be used effectively by those who are unacquainted with Greek. Robertson was one of the finest Greek scholars in his day. No pastor can afford to be without this set. Evangelical.

WUEST, KENNETH SAMUEL. **The New Testament.** 4 vols. Grand Rapids: Wm. B. Eerdmans Publishing Co., 1961.

Wuest was an extremely practical writer. This set is especially helpful for those who do not have a working knowledge of the Greek text. For an older work, see also, Johann A. Bengel, **New Testament Commentary,** 2 vols., Kregel Publications, 1970.

NEW TESTAMENT LANGUAGE TOOLS

GOODRICK, EDWARD W. **Do It Yourself Hebrew and Greek.** Grand Rapids: Zondervan Publishing House, 1980.

In this practical work, the author introduces the alphabets and basic elements of Greek and Hebrew grammar. This book will help a minister or student to use some basic language tools, including analyticals, lexicons, interlinears, concordances, and commentaries.

GREEN, JAY P. **The Interlinear Greek-English New Testament.** Massachusetts: Hendrickson Publishers, 1985.

This is a companion volume to **The Interlinear Old Testament** by Green. The Strong's numbering of each Greek word is placed above the word, thus providing on one page the original word, its Strong's number and a literal English translation for each Greek word, plus a literal English translation in verse-by-verse format parallel to the Interlinear. Its use will allow the novice pastor or student to read the original text without losing too much time looking up the words in a Greek lexicon.

THAYER, JOSEPH HENRY. **The New Thayer's Greek-English Lexicon of the New Testament.** Massachusetts: Hendrickson Publishers, 1981.

This new lexicon has been coded to the numbering system from Strong's Concordance thus allowing those who do not know Greek ready access to this valuable lexicon. Definitions of each word are given, in addition to noting significant occurrences of the word in the New Testament and other Greek literature. See also, William Frederick Arndt and F. Wilber Gingrich, **Greek-English Lexicon of the New Testament,** University of Chicago Press, 1957.

WIGRAM, G. W. **The New Englishman's Greek Concordance and Lexicon.** Massachusetts: Hendrickson Publishers, 1982.

This important work is indexed to: **Strong's Concordance** (numbering system); **Arndt-Gingrich Greek-English Lexicon** (page number); **Kittel's Theological Dictionary** (volume, page number); **Thayer's Greek-English Lexicon** (page column). Since every word is coded to Strong's Concordance, this allows those who do not know Greek the opportunity to utilize this work.

COMMENTARIES ON THE ENTIRE NEW TESTAMENT

BARCLAY, WILLIAM. **Daily Study Bible.** 18 vols. Revised Edition. Philadelphia: Westminster Press, 1985.

These expositional studies are outstanding. They are rich in devotional thought and exegetical insights. Barclay gives his own translation of the entire New Testament arranged in brief passages, followed by his own commentary on each passage. Unfortunately, one cannot accept some of Barclay's theology.

LENSKI, RICHARD CHARLES HENRY. **Interpretation of the New Testament.** 14 volumes. Minneapolis: Augsburg Publishing House, 1946.

You do not have to be a Greek scholar to benefit greatly

from Lenski. Here is a conservative Lutheran writer that knows how to write Biblical exposition. This extensive set is written from the Arminian theological point of view. Amillennial.

INDIVIDUAL COMMENTARIES ON NEW TESTAMENT BOOKS
THE GOSPELS: GENERAL WORKS

FAIRWEATHER, WILLIAM. **The Background of the Gospels.** Minneapolis: Klock and Klock Christian Publishers, 1984.

Fairweather in this older study, traces historically and religiously the interval beginning with the Maccabaean revolt and ending with the destruction of Jerusalem. This book is a result of the author's appointment to the Cunningham lectureship in 1907.

HASTINGS, JAMES, ed. **Dictionary of Christ and the Gospels.** 2 vols. New York: Charles Scribner's Sons, 1907–9.

Of all the well-known Bible Dictionaries edited by Hastings, his Dictionary of Christ and the Gospels is the most valuable. This classic set is loaded with great preaching material about the many aspects of the Life of Christ and the Gospels. It contains over 2000 subjects. This work has now been printed by Baker Book House.

JUKES, ANDREW JOHN. **Four Views of Christ.** Grand Rapids: Kregel Publications, 1982.

Jukes' account of the four gospels is a classic. He shows the characteristic differences in each of the four Gospels. He tackles problems as to why there are differences and how one can apply those differences.

SCROGGIE, WILLIAM GRAHAM. **Guide to the Gospels.** London: Pickering and Inglis, 1962.

This valuable work was first published in 1948 and contains over 670 pages. Scroggie examines each Gospel individually and then proceeds to show their relationship to each other.

TRENCH, RICHARD CHENEVIX. **Studies in the Gospels.**
3d ed., revised. Grand Rapids: Baker Book House, 1979.
Here is a classic work first published in 1886. This revision
includes character studies, history and doctrine. Trench was
an outstanding Anglican scholar.

GOSPEL HARMONIES

ROBERSTON, ARCHIBALD THOMAS. **A Harmony of
the Gospels.** New York: Harper and Brothers, 1922.
In four columns, the writings of Matthew, Mark, Luke, and
John are presented side by side. This work has become a clas-
sic. Be sure and get the thoroughly revised, rearranged and
enlarged edition. For a more up-to-date work, see also, Ralph
Harris, **The Complete Biblical Library,** Gospel Publishing
House, 1986.

MIRACLES

BRUCE, ALEXANDER BALMAIN. **The Miracles of
Christ.** Minneapolis: Klock and Klock Christian Publishers,
1980.
This 532 page classic work demonstrates the miraculous ele-
ment of Christ's ministry and shows how it relates to the pur-
pose, meaning and scope of His Messianic Kingdom program.
The book is valuable from an apologetic standpoint and con-
tains much valuable preaching material.
CHAPPELL, CLOVIS G. **Sermons from the Miracles.** New
York: Abingdon Press, 1969.
These are some of the most practical sermons on the mira-
cles of Christ in print today, by an outstanding Methodist
pastor.
HABERSHON, ADA RUTH. **The Study of the Miracles.**
Grand Rapids: Kregel Publications, 1957.
Habershon takes a premillennial study of the Miracles. The
author reveals the reasons for the Miracles and their applica-
tion for daily life. Conservative.

LAIDLAW, JOHN. **The Miracles of Our Lord.** Grand Rapids: Baker Book House, 1956.

This valuable work was first printed in 1900. It has now become an expositional classic on the Miracles of Jesus Christ.

TAYLOR, WILLIAM MACKERGO. **Miracles of Our Saviour.** Grand Rapids: Kregel Publications, 1975.

Taylor was an outstanding expository preacher. These messages are loaded with homiletical material. Every pastor will consult Taylor again and again for practical material on the Miracles.

TRENCH, RICHARD CHENEVIX. **Notes on the Miracles of Our Lord.** Grand Rapids: Baker Book House, 1979.

This is one of the most comprehensive scriptural studies of the miracles. Even though this work was first published in 1846, it is still helpful for the pastor and Bible student.

PARABLES

ARNOT, WILLIAM. **The Parables of Our Lord.** Grand Rapids: Kregel Publications, 1981.

Here is a concise practical study of the 30 most widely-known parables of Christ. Every pastor will find a lot of helpful devotional material in these 532 pages.

————. **Lesser Parables of Our Lord.** Grand Rapids: Kregel Publications, 1981.

Here is a classic on the lesser-known parables. One will discover the varied theological and biblical concepts embedded in these parables. In addition, there are 26 studies from the book of First Peter as well as 10 lessons of grace illustrated from nature. The final section is entitled, "The Life of Christ."

BRUCE, ALEXANDER BALMAIN. **The Parables of Christ.** Minneapolis: Klock and Klock Christian Publishers, 1980.

This critical study deals with the Parabolic elements of Christ's ministry and shows how they relate to the purpose, meaning and scope of His Messianic Kingdom program. This classic work contains some 391 pages.

CHAPPELL, CLOVIS G. **Sermons from the Parables.** New York: Abingdon Press, 1969.

The best word to describe this work is practical. Chappell's sermons on the Parables will give any minister a lot of homiletical hints for sermon preparation.

KEACH, BENJAMIN. **Exposition of the Parables.** Grand Rapids: Kregel Publications, 1974.

Here is a thorough exposition of every parable spoken by Jesus Christ. In this series of 147 messages on all the parables and similitudes spoken by Christ in the Four Gospels, Keach not only instructs people into practical Christian living, but also expounds great doctrinal truths. This volume contains 918 pages.

MORGAN, GEORGE CAMPBELL. **The Parables and Metaphors of Our Lord.** Westwood, N.J.: Fleming H. Revell Co., 1943.

This exposition is probably one of Morgan's greatest works. Every preacher will want this important study on the Parables and Metaphors of Christ. For another parabolic work by the same author, see also, **The Parable of the Father's Heart,** Baker Book House, 1968.

TAYLOR, WILLIAM MACKERGO. **Parables of Our Saviour.** Grand Rapids: Kregel Publications, 1975.

For expository preaching ideas on the Parables, this classic reprint is a must. This work is considered to be an extremely practical exposition that offers an evangelistic thrust to the Parables.

TRENCH, RICHARD CHENEVIX. **Notes on the Parables of Our Lord.** Grand Rapids: Baker Book House, 1979.

When it comes to the Parables of Christ, these notes are unsurpassed in their depth of spiritual insight and exposition. Even though this work was first published in 1841, it is still valuable to the minister and Bible student. See also, John Laidlaw, **Studies in the Parables of Our Lord,** Klock and Klock Christian Publishers, 1981.

METAPHORS

FRASER, DONALD. **The Metaphors of Christ.** Minneapolis: Klock and Klock Christian Publishers, 1985.

This work has been out-of-print for several years. Fraser studies the metaphors used by Christ (e.g., "salt of the earth," "light of the world," etc.). There are a lot of helpful illustrations and devotional gems to help in sermon preparation.

KEACH, BENJAMIN. **Preaching from the Types and Metaphors of the Bible.** Grand Rapids: Kregel Publications, 1974.

Every pastor will glean sermonic material from this classical reprint of 1038 pages. Keach gives a complete analysis of the spiritual significance of each type and metaphor along with its practical application for today.

BIBLE CHARACTERS FROM THE GOSPELS

BRUCE, ALEXANDER BALMAIN. **The Training of the Twelve.** Grand Rapids: Kregel Publications, 1971.

Even though this work was first published in 1871, it has never been equaled. This classic, learned, practical and inspiring book on the twelve apostles is a must for every minister's library.

CHAPPELL, CLOVIS G. **Sermons on Simon Peter.** New York: Abingdon Press, 1959.

These are some of the finest sermons on the various aspects of Peter's life in print today. Chappell makes the Bible character of Peter come alive. Practical.

JONES, JOHN DANIEL. **The Apostles of Christ.** Minneapolis: Klock and Klock Christian Publishers, 1981.

Jones was a renown master of the pulpit in his day. This work was formerly published under the title, **The Glorious Company of the Apostles.** Here is an outstanding example of Bible character preaching.

LOANE, MARCUS LAWRENCE. **John the Baptist: As Witness and Martyr.** Grand Rapids: Zondervan Publishing House, 1968.

The author gives an outstanding devotional account of the life and ministry of John the Baptist. This is one of the most revealing accounts of John's ministry.

MACARTNEY, CLARENCE EDWARD NOBLE. **Of Them He Chose Twelve.** Grand Rapids: Baker Book House, 1969.

Macartney was an outstanding preacher on Bible characters. This series of sermons on the twelve apostles radiate with practical truth and Bible exposition.

MACDUFF, JOHN ROSS. **The Footsteps of St. Peter.** Minneapolis: Klock and Klock Christian Publishers, 1981.

MacDuff wrote several outstanding works on Bible characters. This account of the life of Peter was one of his finest expositions. It is a practical work of 648 pages.

MEYER, FREDERICK BROTHERTON. **John the Baptist.** London: Marshall, Morgan and Scott, 1954.

This author was one of the better devotional writers on Bible characters. Here is an excellent example of preaching on the courageous life of John the Baptist.

————. **Peter: Fisherman, Disciple, Apostle.** London: Marshall, Morgan and Scott, 1953.

A practical and devotional study on the life of Peter. Every pastor will want to consult Meyer before preaching a series of messages on Peter.

MORGAN, GEORGE CAMPBELL. **The Great Physician.** Westwood, N.J.: Fleming H. Revell Co., 1963.

This outstanding work shows the method that Jesus used in dealing with the various Bible characters in the Gospels and Acts. It is loaded with homiletical material.

ROBERTSON, ARCHIBALD THOMAS. **Epochs in the Life of Simon Peter.** New York: Charles Scribner's Sons, 1933.

Robertson demonstrates great insight in his studies on Bible characters. This work on the life, ministry, and writings of Peter is an excellent example. Now in paperback from Broadman Press.

————. **Epochs in the Life of the Apostle John.** New York: Charles Scribner's Sons, 1935.

In this series of studies in the life of John the Apostle, Robertson outlines the ministry and writings of this beloved Bible character. Now in print in paperback from Broadman Press. For an excellent study on Mark, see also, Archibald T. Robertson, **Making Good in the Ministry,** Broadman Press, 1959.

————. **John the Loyal: Studies in the Ministry of John the Baptist.** Grand Rapids: Baker Book House, 1977.

This is not one of Robertson's better works on Bible characters, but it is still helpful in sermon preparation for a series of messages on John the Baptist.

THOMAS, WILLIAM HENRY GRIFFITH. **The Apostle Peter: Outline Studies in His Life, Character and Writings.** Grand Rapids: Wm. B. Eerdmans Publishing Co., 1950.

This work is excellent for devotional study or homiletical use. These outline studies include each event in Peter's life and every verse or chapter in his Epistles. Now in paperback from Kregel Publications.

————. **The Apostle John: Studies in His Life and Writings.** Grand Rapids: Wm. B. Eerdmans Publishing Co., 1946.

This outline study is loaded with great teaching and preaching material. Thomas outlines each period and event in the life of John, his Gospel, his three Epistles, and the Book of Revelation. Now in paperback from Kregel Publications.

THE GOSPELS

MORGAN, GEORGE CAMPBELL. **Studies in the Four Gospels.** New Jersey: Fleming H. Revell Co., 1927.

Morgan's studies in the four gospels are among his best known works. This study of Matthew, Mark, Luke and John is rich in interpretation, suggestion and application. For those who want a larger print, this work can also be purchased in 4 volumes by the same publisher.

RYLE, JOHN CHARLES. **Expository Thoughts on the Gospels.** 7 vols. London: James Clarke and Co. Ltd., 1956.

Even though this set was first issued in 1856, it is still in great demand. Ryle was an extremely practical preacher. This work is one of his best. Devotional. This set can also be purchased in 4 volumes and in paperback form.

MATTHEW

ALEXANDER, JOSEPH ADDISON. **The Gospel According to Matthew.** Lynchburg, VA: James Family Publishing Co., 1979.

Unfortunately, Alexander died before he completed this work on the Gospel of Matthew. This excellent commentary only covers the first 16 chapters of Matthew. Alexander was not afraid to tackle problem passages.

BROADUS, JOHN ALBERT. **Commentary on the Gospel of Matthew.** Philadelphia: American Baptist Publication Society, 1886.

This work contains a detailed introduction, expositions, and a wealth of homiletical and practical notes. Broadus takes an Amillennial approach in explaining the Olivet discourse. Judson Press has now published this book by Broadus.

HENDRICKSEN, WILLIAM. **Exposition of the Gospel According to Matthew.** New Testament Commentary. Grand Rapids: Baker Book House, 1973.

Hendricksen uses the Greek language in a manner that can be easily understood by any minister. This work has a thorough introduction to Matthew and presents materials not usually found in other commentaries. Calvinistic. For another good expository commentary, although slightly liberal, see also, Alfred Plummer, **An Exegetical Commentary on the Gospel According to St. Matthew,** Baker Book House, 1984.

KELLY, WILLIAM. **Lectures on the Gospel of Matthew.** New York: Loizeaux Brothers, 1959.

Although these lectures were first published in 1868, they are still valuable today. Kelly was a well-known British Bible teacher who made an excellent contribution to evangelical scholarship.

MORISON, JAMES. **The Gospel According to Matthew.** Minneapolis: Klock and Klock Christian Publishers, 1981.

Dr. Morison was an outstanding expository preacher who influenced the spiritual awakening in several parts of Scotland in the 1800's. This excellent devotional phrase by phrase commentary on Matthew contains 706 pages.

MORRISON, GEORGE H. **Matthew.** 3 vols. Chattanooga, TN: AMG Publishers, 1978.

This older work is noted for its forceful and practical material. These expository sermons on the Book of Matthew will aid any minister in homiletical preparation. For a more up-to-date homiletical commentary on Matthew, see also, John MacArthur, **The MacArthur New Testament Commentary: Matthew,** Moody Press, 1985.

THOMAS, WILLIAM HENRY GRIFFITH. **Outline Studies in the Gospel of Matthew.** Grand Rapids: Wm. B. Eerdmans Publishing Co., 1961.

This work by Thomas is both homiletical and expository. In sixty studies, the author presents in outline form and with practical applications the truths of Matthew's Gospel. Kregel Publications has now printed this work in paperback. For a good more up-to-date expository work from a Mennonite pastor, see also, Myron Augsburger, **Matthew: The Communicator's Commentary,** Word Books, 1984.

SERMON ON THE MOUNT

CHAPPELL, CLOVIS G. **Sermon on the Mount.** New York: Abingdon Press, n.d.

If one is looking for homiletical material for a series of messages on The Sermon on the Mount, these sermons by Chappell will be extremely helpful and practical. Now in paperback from Baker Book House. For more detailed homiletical material, see also, James Montgomery Boice, **The Sermon on the Mount,** Zondervan Publishing House, 1972.

LLOYD-JONES, DAVID MARTYN. **Studies in the Sermon on the Mount.** 2 vols. Grand Rapids: Wm. B. Eerdmans Publishing Co., 1959–60.

This set is a brilliant and detailed exposition of the Sermon on the Mount. It is homiletical and devotional in character, and a treasury of spiritual truths. Now available in one volume.

MEYER, FEDERICK BROTHERTON. **The Directory of the Devout Life.** New Jersey: Fleming H. Revell Co., 1904.

Although these meditations on the Sermon on the Mount are brief, Meyer allows the reader to follow the Master's steps as He ascended to the mountain and calls men out of sin into a devoted life. Devotional.

PINK, ARTHUR WALKINGTON. **An Exposition of the Sermon on the Mount.** Grand Rapids: Baker Book House, 1951.

This devotional and expositional commentary of the Sermon on the Mount consists of 64 chapters. It is thorough, helpful, practical and shows how pertinently and pointedly this sermon applies to us today.

STOTT, JOHN ROBERT WALMSEY. **Christian Counter-Culture: The Message of the Sermon on the Mount.** Downers Grove, IL: Inter-Varsity Press, 1978.

Stott offers a careful and accurate exposition of Matthew 5–7 and relates it vividly to life today. For another helpful expository study, see also, John D. Pentecost, **The Sermon on the Mount: Contemporary Insights for a Christian Lifestyle,** Multnomah Press, 1980.

THE BEATITUDES

MEYER, FREDERICK BROTHERTON. **Blessed Are Ye: Talks on the Beatitudes.** Grand Rapids: Baker Book House, 1955.

The beatitudes come alive in this rich devotional study. Of course, a minister should strive for both exposition and devotion in his sermon preparation. In this study, Meyer gives one a balance of both.

MACARTHUR, JOHN, JR. **Kingdom Living Here and Now.** Chicago: Moody Press, 1980.

MacArthur's expository works are getting more in demand

each day. If a minister wants to see how one expositor handles the Beatitudes, this is the book to buy.

WIERSBE, WARREN W. **Live Like a King: Making the Beatitudes Work in Daily Life.** Chicago: Moody Press, 1976.

Wiersbe has written extensively on homiletical literature. This devotional work explains each beatitude in a separate chapter, draws modern-day parallels, and makes practical applications.

THE LORD'S PRAYER

CHAPPELL, CLOVIS G. **Sermons on the Lord's Prayer.** Nashville: Cokesbury Press, 1934.

It is hard to believe that so many writer's of books on the minister's library overlook many of Chappell's writings. These sermons on the Lord's Prayer by Chappell are excellent. In addition, he writes on the other prayers of Jesus in this book.

REDPATH, ALAN. **Victorious Praying.** Westwood, N.J.: Fleming H. Revell Co., 1957.

Redpath preaches as he writes. This would be an excellent book to use as a helpful guide in preparing a series of messages on the Lord's Prayer.

SAPHIR, ADOLPH. **Our Lord's Pattern for Prayer.** Grand Rapids: Kregel Publications, 1984.

This classic reprint is a thorough work on "The Lord's Prayer." It will be difficult to find a more complete and exegetical book than Saphir on this important study. Each section is systematically outlined for ease of understanding. Practical.

MARK

ALEXANDER, JOSEPH ADDISON. **Commentary on the Gospel of Mark.** Minneapolis: Klock and Klock Christian Publishers, 1980.

This classic reprint is one of the best older works on the Gospel of Mark. Alexander gives a good defense of Mark as an independent witness to the life of Christ.

COLE, ROBERT ALAN. **The Gospel According to St. Mark.** Tyndale New Testament Commentaries. Grand Rapids: Wm. B. Eerdmans Publishing Co., 1961.

Even though this work is not detailed, it is helpful because of its expositional and exegetical value. Cole is an outstanding evangelical author. For other expositional works on Mark, see also, Ray C. Stedman, **The Servant Who Rules and The Ruler Who Serves,** Zondervan Publishing House, 1976.

HENDRICKSEN, WILLIAM. **Exposition of the Gospel According to Mark.** New Testament Commentary. Grand Rapids: Baker Book House, 1975.

Every minister will want to consult Hendricksen every time they preach or teach from Mark's Gospel. This work is clear, complete, easy to read, and Biblical. Hendricksen's footnotes are also helpful.

LANE, WILLIAM L. **The Gospel According to Mark.** New International Commentary on the New Testament. Grand Rapids: Wm. B. Eerdmans Publishing Co., 1974.

This is a helpful recent work on the Gospel of Mark. It is exegetical and yet it has many devotional values that enhance the value of this book. Special notes and footnotes are also included. For another more scholarly approach, see also, Henry B. Swete, **Commentary on Mark,** Kregel Publications, 1977.

MORISON, JAMES. **The Gospel According to Mark.** Minneapolis: Klock and Klock Christian Publishers, 1981.

This devotional work is a companion volume to Morison's commentary on Matthew. When a minister decides to preach or teach a series of messages on a book of the Bible, he will always want to consult some of the classic older works such as this one by Morison. For another good devotional work, see also, William G. Scroggie, **The Gospel of Mark,** Zondervan Publishing House, 1976.

OGILVIE, LLOYD JOHN. **Life Without Limits: the Message of Mark's Gospel.** Waco, TX: Word Books, 1975.

If one is looking for good preaching material on Mark, this work by Ogilvie will be helpful. The author uses the Gospel of Mark to stress the importance of discipleship. For other good homiletical helps, see also, George H. Morrison, **Mark,** AMG Publishers, 1978.

ROBERTSON, ARCHIBALD THOMAS. **Studies in Mark's Gospel.** Revised and edited by Herber F. Peacock. Nashville: Broadman Press, 1958.

In the first three chapters of this book, Robertson deals with John Mark as a person, the date of the Gospel, and its relation to Matthew and Luke. The final four chapters discuss the person and work of Christ. This work is written as a practical guide for an overview study of Mark rather than a verse-by-verse commentary.

LUKE

GELDENHUYS, JOHANNES NORVAL. **Commentary on the Gospel of Luke.** New International Commentary on the New Testament. Grand Rapids: Wm. B. Eerdmans Publishing Co., 1951.

This commentary on the Gospel of Luke is well documented, unusually extensive and makes good use of New Testament expository literature. It is both practical and critical. A work of massive scholarship.

GODET, FREDERICK LOUIS. **Commentary on Luke.** Grand Rapids: Kregel Publications, 1981.

This work is a classic reprint that was first published in 1870. A minister needs to read Godet slowly, but the rewards are worth the extra effort. All of his commentaries have now become standard works in the field of biblical exposition.

HENDRICKSEN, WILLIAM. **Exposition of the Gospel According to Luke.** New Testament Commentary. Grand Rapids: Baker Book House, 1974.

Of all the commentaries that Hendricksen wrote, this one on the gospel of Luke is probably the best. For more information on Hendricksen's works, look under Matthew and Mark.

KELLY, WILLIAM. **The Gospel of Luke.** Minneapolis: Klock and Klock Christian Publishers, 1981.

This classic reprint contains some sound evangelical exposition of Luke's Gospel. Kelly has mastered the theme of Luke and the original text in an extremely helpful manner.

MORRIS, LEON. **The Gospel According to St. Luke.** Tyndale New Testament Commentaries. Grand Rapids: Wm. B. Eerdmans Publishing Co., 1974.

The value of this work lies primarily in its exegetical research and recent scholarship. In addition, Morris gives a lot of good background material in his introduction. For another good expositional, evangelical work, see also, William F. Arndt, **Gospel According to St. Luke.** Concordia Publishing House, 1956.

MORRISON, GEORGE H. **Luke.** 2 vols. Chattanooga, TN: AMG Publishers, 1978.

For some rich homiletical material on Luke's Gospel, Morrison will be extremely helpful. This work is not a verse-by-verse commentary.

ROBERTSON, ARCHIBALD THOMAS. **Luke the Historian in the Light of Research.** Nashville: Broadman Press, 1978.

This work is not a verse-by-verse commentary. In this book, Robertson defends the authenticity of Luke's gospel and ably throws new light on the life and times of the early church.

STRONSTAD, ROGER, **The Charismatic Theology of St. Luke.** Peabody, MA: Hendrickson Publishers, 1986.

This work is a significant contribution regarding the meaning of the Holy Spirit's activity in Luke–Acts. Stronstad challenges traditional protestants to re-examine and reconsider the impact of Pentecost. Pentecostal/Charismatic.

THOMAS, WILLIAM HENRY GRIFFITH. **Outline Studies in the Gospel of Luke.** Grand Rapids: Wm. B. Eerdmans Publishing Co., 1950.

Thomas developed these practical sermon outlines from his personal devotional life. It is not a verse-by-verse section outline of Luke's Gospel. This work is now published in paperback by Kregel Publications.

JOHN

BOICE, JAMES MONTGOMERY. **The Gospel of John.**
Grand Rapids: Zondervan Publishing House, 1986.

Boice is an outstanding expository preacher. His books reflect thorough research and rank among some of the best for good examples of exposition. This work on John is a massive treatise of homiletical material. For another good older homiletical work, see also, George H. Morrison, **John,** AMG Publishers, 1978.

GODET, FREDERICK LOUIS. **Commentary on John's Gospel.** Grand Rapids: Kregel Publications, 1978.

This exhaustive English treatment of John's Gospel was first published in 1893. From a theological and Christological standpoint, Godet has written one of the best works available in print today.

HENDRICKSEN, WILLIAM. **Exposition of the Gospel According to John.** New Testament Commentary. Grand Rapids: Baker Book House, 1953.

For a detailed study of words, doctrines and other important aspects of John, Hendricksen's work on John's Gospel is extremely helpful. Evangelical and reformed.

HENGSTENBERG, ERNST WILHELM. **A Commentary on the Gospel of St. John.** 2 vols. Minneapolis: Klock and Klock Christian Publishers, 1980.

In this well-balanced massive commentary on John's Gospel, Hengstenberg develops the life and works of Christ brilliantly from the Apostle's writings. This work is a classic reprint.

MORRIS, LEON L. **The Gospel According to John.** New International Commentary on the New Testament. Grand Rapids: Wm. B. Eerdmans Publishing Co., 1971.

This expository commentary on John's Gospel is extremely valuable for recent scholarship. It also contains a valuable introduction, special notes, complete expositions, and valuable footnotes. For another expository work, see also, Brooke F. Westcott, **The Gospel According to St. John,** Wm. B. Eerdmans Publishing Co., 1950.

PINK, ARTHUR WALKINGTON. **Exposition of the Gospel of John.** 3 vols. Grand Rapids: Zondervan Publishing House, 1945.

This devotional commentary on John's Gospel is loaded with homiletical ideas for the minister. Pink is a strong Calvinistic writer, but this work is worth having.

TENNEY, MERRILL CHAPIN. **John: The Gospel of Belief.** Grand Rapids: Wm. B. Eerdmans Publishing Co., 1948.

In this work, Tenney gives one superb analytical study of the text of John's Gospel. This is not a verse-by-verse commentary. It is an overview study of the unity and theology of the Gospel as a whole. See also, Archibald T. Robertson, **Divinity of Christ in the Gospel of John,** Broadman Press, 1976.

JOHN 15

ROSSCUP, JAMES E. **Abiding in Christ: Studies in John 15.** Grand Rapids: Zondervan Publishing House, 1973.

This thorough treatment of John 15:1–6 will assist any minister in preparing a series of expository messages on this subject. Practical.

STEDMAN, RAY C. **Secrets of the Spirit.** Old Tappen, NJ: Fleming H. Revell, CO., 1975.

Stedman is a good expository preacher. In this series of messages on John 14–17, the author deals with the events just prior to the crucifixion. Homiletical. For another good work, see also, Thomas D. Bernard, **The Central Teaching of Christ,** Klock and Klock Christian Publishers, 1981.

JOHN 17

BROWN, JOHN. **Exposition of Our Lord's Intercessory Prayer.** Minneapolis: Klock and Klock Christian Publishers, 1979.

Even though this work on John 17 was first printed in 1866, it is still a valuable exposition. Brown deals with the Lord's high-priestly prayer thoroughly and systematically. For another similar work, see also, Thomas Manton, **An Exposition of John 17,** Sovereign Grace Book Club, 1958.

RAINSFORD, MARCUS. **Our Lord Prays for His Own.** Chicago: Moody Press, 1950.

These extensive studies on John 17 are timely, relevant and devotional. This work is considered to be one of the greatest classics ever written on Christ's high priestly prayer. This work is now in paperback from Kregel Publications.

ACTS

ALEXANDER, JOSEPH ADDISON. **Commentary on the Acts of the Apostles.** 2 vols. in 1. Minneapolis: Klock and Klock Christian Publishers, 1980.

The main concern of this author is to promote an exhaustive understanding of the text of Acts and of its message as a whole. Most of the practical application is left to the preacher or discerning reader. Reformed.

BRUCE, FREDERICK FYVIE. **Commentary on the Book of Acts.** New International Commentary on the New Testament. Grand Rapids: Wm. B. Eerdmans Publishing Co., 1954.

This valuable commentary on the Book of Acts contains the English text with an introduction, exposition and notes. Bruce is an excellent writer and is fully acquainted with the most recent New Testament research. Expository. For a good historical commentary on Acts, see also, William M. Ramsey, **Pictures of the Apostolic Church,** Baker Book House, 1959.

CHAPPELL, CLOVIS G. **When the Church Was Young.** New York: Abingdon Press, 1950.

Chappell's practical sermons demonstrate that the solution to the problems our churches face today can be found in the Book of Acts. This is not a verse-by-verse commentary. For another example of good sermons, see also, William Arnot, **Studies in Acts: The Church in the House,** Kregel Publications, 1978.

GLOAG, PATON JAMES. **A Critical and Exegetical Com-**

mentary on the Acts of the Apostles. 2 vols. Minneapolis: Klock and Klock Christian Publishers, 1979.

This thorough exposition on the book of Acts shows a lot of research by an older Scottish Presbyterian minister. The author was not afraid to tackle any problems in the text.

HASTINGS, JAMES, ed. **Dictionary of the Apostolic Church.** 2 vols. New York: Charles Scribner's Sons, 1963.

Even though this work is not a verse-by-verse commentary on the Book of Acts, it contains a dictionary that covers the history of the Christian church as detailed in Acts through Revelation to the end of the first century. Some articles have some liberal tendencies, but basically the work is composed of good solid background material. Now available from Baker Book House.

MORGAN, GEORGE CAMPBELL. **The Acts of the Apostles.** New York: Fleming H. Revell Co., 1924.

Morgan's commentary on the Book of Acts demonstrates his keen insight into the Scriptures. He gives readers a vivid, persuasive understanding of Christianity's early days as reflected in the Acts. Expository. For a good work on Acts 2, see also, George C. Morgan, **The Birth of the Church,** Fleming H. Revell Co., 1968.

OGILVIE, LLOYD JOHN. **ACTS.** The Communicator's Commentary. Waco, TX: Word Books, 1984.

Of all the authors in this set, Ogilvie's work on the Book of Acts is one of the best. He is also the general editor of this series. For a good work of great homiletical help on the Book of Acts, see also, Lloyd J. Ogilvie, **The Drumbeat of Love,** Word Books, 1976.

RACKHAM, RICHARD BELWARD. **The Acts of the Apostles.** Grand Rapids: Baker Book House, 1964.

This extensive commentary was first published in 1901. It is a valuable exposition written in a clear and understandable way. Rackham interprets the meaining of the Book of Acts to the present generation. Expository. This work is now in paperback by Baker Book House.

TOURVILLE, ROBERT E. **The Acts of the Apostles.** New Wilmington, PA: House of Bon Giovanni, 1983.

This verse-by-verse commentary on the Book of Acts is a product of many years of study. The author shows careful research in this devotional and expositional work. Pentecostal/ Charismatic. For another smaller pentecostal work, see also Stanley, M. Horton, **The Book of Acts,** The Radiant Commentary on the New Testament, Gospel Publishing House, 1981.

THOMAS, WILLIAM HENRY GRIFFITH. **Outline Studies in the Acts of the Apostles.** Grand Rapids: Wm. B. Eerdmans Publishing Co., 1956.

It is important to keep in mind that this is not a verse-by-verse commentary. This work has a lot of homiletical suggestions in outline form. These studies are rich, and filled with practical application.

VAUGHAN, CHARLES JOHN. **Studies in the Book of Acts.** Minneapolis: Klock and Klock Christian Publishers, 1981.

The works of C. J. Vaughan have been neglected for years. These expository messages on the Book of Acts contain some outstanding examples of good Biblical preaching. For another good older work, see also, Rudolf E. Stier, **Words of the Apostles,** Klock and Klock Christian Publishers, 1981.

THE LIFE OF PAUL

BRUCE, FREDERICK FYVIE. **Paul: Apostle of the Heart Set Free.** Grand Rapids: Wm. B. Eerdmans Publishing Co., 1977.

This work on Paul's life is valuable because it represents Bruce's lifetime study of the Pauline Epistles. In this up-to-date study, Bruce deals with history, archaeology, and other related background material on the life of Paul.

EADIE, JOHN. **The Words of the Apostle Paul.** Minneapolis: Klock and Klock Christian Publishers, 1981.

The reissue of this study will be valuable to all who seek to understand Paul's discourses and speeches as contained in the Book of Acts. Eadie clearly demonstrates some of the secrets of the early church's dynamic witness.

ROBERTSON, ARCHIBALD THOMAS. **Epochs in the Life of Paul.** New York: Charles Scribner's Sons, 1937.

Several of Robertson's works are now being reprinted. This work will be helpful for the minister who would like to preach a series of messages on the Life of Paul. Now this work can be purchased in paperback from Broadman Press. For another work on Paul, by the same author, see also, Archibald T. Robertson, **Paul, the Interpreter of Christ,** Broadman Press, 1978.

STALKER, JAMES. **The Life of Paul.** Westwood, N.J.: Fleming H. Revell Co., 1950.

For a brief, classic treatment of the life of Paul, Stalker is a must. It is both informative and heartwarming. This is a good solid handbook on Paul's life. For a more up-to-date and extensive study on Paul's life, see also, Reginald E. O. White, **Apostle Extraordinary: A Modern Portrait of St. Paul,** Wm. B. Eerdmans Publishing Co., 1962.

TAYLOR, WILLIAM MACKERO. **Paul the Missionary.** Grand Rapids: Baker Book House, 1962.

Taylor's work on Paul's life is a classic. This valuable reprint of the 1909 edition will be extremely helpful to the minister that is looking for homiletical material on the life of Paul. For a brief devotional study of Paul's life, see also, Frederick B. Meyer, **Paul: A Servant of Jesus Christ,** Christian Literature Crusade, 1978.

PAULINE EPISTLES

CONEYBEARE, WILLIAM JOHN AND JOHN SAUL HOWSON. **The Life and Epistles of Paul.** Grand Rapids: Wm. B. Eerdmans Publishing Co., 1953.

Even though this thorough work was first published in 1852, it is still a classic worth consulting. It has long been the standard introduction to Paul's life and letters. For another older work on the Epistles of Paul, see also, William Fairweather, **The Background of the Epistles,** Klock and Klock Christian Publishers, 1977.

GODET, FREDERICK LOUIS. **Studies in Paul's Epistles.** Grand Rapids: Kregel Publications, 1984.

Even though this work was written several years ago, it is still helpful. It is a remarkable treatise on the Epistles of Paul. This work is a classic and contains many excellent discussions. For another good work, see also, Joseph B. Lightfoot, **Notes on the Epistles of Paul,** Alpha Publications, 1979.

HIEBERT, DAVID EDMOND. **An Introduction to the Pauline Epistles.** Chicago: Moody Press, 1954.

This up-to-date evangelical work presents a comprehensive and scholarly study of the Pauline Epistles. In addition, it covers basic introductory and historical material.

MACHEN, JOHN GRESHAM, **The Origin of Paul's Religion.** Grand Rapids: Wm. B. Eerdmans Publishing Co., 1970.

Machen, was a tremendous New Testament writer. He delivered these lectures years ago, defending Paul's teachings about the person and work of Jesus Christ. It is an outstanding work in Christian evidences. Amillennial. For another excellent older work, see also, James S. Stewart, **A Man in Christ: The Vital Elements in Paul's Religion,** Harper and Row, 1935.

RAMSEY, WILLIAM MITCHELL. **St. Paul the Traveller and the Roman Citizen.** Grand Rapids: Baker Book House, 1960.

This work is especially valuable for historical and archaeological background. For two other important works, see also, William M. Ramsey, **Pauline and Other Studies in Early Christian History,** Baker Book House, 1970 and William M. Ramsey, **The Cities of St. Paul,** Baker Book House, 1960.

ROMANS

BROWN, JOHN. **Analytical Exposition of the Epistle of Paul the Apostle to the Romans.** Klock and Klock Christian Publishers, 1979.

Even though this exposition was written in 1857, Brown had a depth and understanding of the Bible that makes him a master commentator. For another good, older Puritan reformed commentary, see also, Robert Haldane, **Exposition of the Epistle to the Romans,** Banner of Truth Trust, reprint.

GODET, FREDERICK LOUIS. **Commentary on St. Paul's Epistle to the Romans.** Grand Rapids: Zondervan Publishing House, 1970.

The primary aim of this commentary is exegetical and theological. Godet is known as the best French Commentator and his work on Romans is a true classic. In addition, this fine expository treatment can be used for homiletical purposes. For another older work that was originally printed in the **Expositor's Bible,** see also, H. C. G. Moule, **The Epistle to the Romans,** Klock and Klock Christian Publishers, 1978.

HENDRICKSEN, WILLIAM. **Exposition of Paul's Epistle to the Romans.** New Testament Commentary. Grand Rapids: Baker Book House, 1980.

This massive work is now in one volume. Hendricksen completed this commentary just before his death. He used all the latest research in producing this excellent exposition on Paul's Epistle. For another recent work, see also, Charles E. B. Cranfield, **Romans: A Shorter Commentary,** Wm. B. Eerdmans Publishing Co., 1986.

LIDDON, HENRY PARRY. **Explanatory Analysis of St. Paul's Epistle to the Romans.** Minneapolis: James and Klock Publishing Co., 1977.

Liddon's exegetical comments on the structure of the text are valuable. These expository studies will prove helpful to a minister preparing to preach a series of sermons on the Book of Romans. For a good smaller work, see also, James M. Stifler, **The Epistle to the Romans,** Moody Press, 1960.

MURRAY, JOHN. **The Epistle to the Romans.** New International Commentary on the New Testament. Grand Rapids: Wm. B. Eerdmans Publishing Co., 1968.

In this exegetical commentary on Romans, Murray has written an inspiring work. The writer has made a significant contribution to conservative biblical scholarship. For another recent work, see also, Frederick F. Bruce, **The Epistle of Paul to the Romans,** Wm. B. Eerdmans Publishing Co., 1963.

SHEDD, WILLIAM GREENOUGH THAYER. **A Critical**

Commentary on the Epistle of St. Paul to the Romans. Minneapolis: Klock and Klock Christian Publishers, 1978.

This classic commentary on Romans was first published in 1879. It is an exegetical commentary written by a reformed theologian. For another classic work, see also, Charles Hodge, **Commentary on the Epistle to the Romans,** Wm. B. Eerdmans Publishing Co., 1950.

STEDMAN, RAY C. **From Guilt to Glory.** 2 vols. Waco, TX: Word Books, 1978.

For a good example of recent expository preaching on Romans, Stedman is a must. These volumes are relevant and devotional. For another excellent example of expository preaching, see also, David Martyn Lloyd-Jones, **Romans,** Zondervan Publishing House, 1971–1976.

THOMAS, WILLIAM HENRY GRIFFITH. **St. Paul's Epistle to the Romans.** Grand Rapids: Wm. B. Eerdmans Publishing Co., 1970.

In this work, Thomas shows careful scholarship, exegetical insight and spiritual application. This devotional commentary will give any minister a lot of rich, homiletical material in sermon preparation.

ROMANS 8

NEE, WATCHMAN [pseud.]. **The Normal Christian Life.** Fort Washington, Penn.: Christian Literature Crusade, 1961.

Nee covers Romans 8 and other certain key passages in the Epistle to the Romans. This work is extremely practical, but it takes slow reading. For a more extensive work, on Romans 8, see, Marcus L. Loane, **The Hope of Glory.** London: Hodder and Stoughton, 1968.

WOOD, ARTHUR SKELVINGTON. **Life by the Spirit.** Grand Rapids: Zondervan Publishing House, 1956.

In this work, Wood has delivered some excellent expository messages on Romans 8. For another good expository work, see also, John Robert Walmsey Stott, **Men Made New,** Inter-Varsity Fellowship, 1966.

FIRST CORINTHIANS

BARRETT, CHARLES KINGSLEY. **A Commentary on the First Epistle to the Corinthians.** Harper's New Testament Commentaries. New York: Harper and Row: 1968.

Barrett's work on the Epistle of Paul to the Corinthians is one of the better works in this series of commentaries. This is a good exegetical commentary, but one has to reject his views on the inspiration of Scripture. Liberal. For a good evangelical, exegetical commentary, see also, Archibald Robertson and Alfred Plummer, **A Critical and Exegetical Commentary on the First Epistle of St. Paul to the Corinthians.** 2d ed., T. and T. Clark, 1914.

EDWARDS, THOMAS CHARLES. **A Commentary on the First Epistle to the Corinthians.** Minneapolis: Klock and Klock Christian Publishers, 1979.

This exegetical commentary by Edwards uses the Greek text. But one can still use this work without having a knowledge of the Greek language. Even though this is an older commentary, it is still a rich verse-by-verse, conservative exposition.

GODET, FREDERICK LOUIS. **Commentary on the First Epistle of St. Paul to the Corinthians.** Translated by A. Cousins. Grand Rapids: Zondervan Publishing House, 1957.

Godet's commentary on First Corinthians is one of the best in print today. This book has been reprinted from the 1886 edition. A careful reading of this exegetical work will pay rich dividends. This book is now published by Kregel Publications.

HODGE, CHARLES. **An Exposition of the First Epistle to the Corinthians.** Grand Rapids: Wm. B. Eerdmans Publishing Co., 1965.

This doctrinal commentary was written back in 1857. Even though Hodge has a tendency to be overly Calvinistic in his commentaries, he is still worth consulting for Bible study.

MACARTHUR, JOHN, JR. **First Corinthians: The MacArthur New Testament Commentary.** Chicago: Moody Press, 1985.

For a good homiletical and expositional commentary on

First Corinthians, MacArthur is one of the best. In chapter 15, he is Premillennial in his interpretation of the rapture of the church and the tribulation period. For another good homiletical commentary, see also, Alan Redpath, **The Royal Route to Heaven: Studies in I Corinthians,** Pickering and Inglis, 1960.

MORGAN, GEORGE CAMPBELL. **The Corinthian Letters of Paul.** Westwood, N. J.: Fleming H. Revell Co., 1956.

Although this is not a detailed commentary by Morgan, it is still a valuable expository work on First and Second Corinthians. Morgan's approach is inspirational and informative.

MORRIS, LEON. **The First Epistle of Paul to the Corinthians.** Tyndale New Testament Commentary. Grand Rapids: Wm. B. Eerdmans Publishing Co., 1958.

Not all the volumes in this series on the New Testament are of equal value. This work by Morris is both clear and useful in sermon preparation and Bible study. For a more extensive work, see, F. W. Grosheide, **The First Epistle to the Corinthians,** Wm. B. Eerdmans Publishing Co., 1953.

FIRST CORINTHIANS 12–14

GEE, DONALD. **Concerning Spiritual Gifts.** Springfield, MO.: Gospel Publishing House, 1972.

This important work is a study of the supernatural working of God in the Early Church. The author outlines the ministry of each gift as revealed in First Corinthians 12–14. Pentecostal/ Charismatic. For another good work in this area of study, see also, Harold Horton, **The Gifts of the Spirit,** Gospel Publishing House, 1949.

KYDD, RONALD A. N. **Charismatic Gifts in the Early Church.** Peabody, MA.: Hedrickson Publishers, 1985.

Kydd effectively helps to answer that old question, "Did charismatic gifts cease in the early church?" Dr. Kydd provides an objective and informative analysis of the study. Pentecostal/Charismatic.

MACDONALD, WILLIAM G. **Glossolalia in the New Testament.** Springfield, MO.: Gospel Publishing House, n.d.

This brief, but informative book deals with the study of glossolalia as found in Luke's account of the first Pentecost. In addition, he deals with the distinction between personal glossolalia and the glossolalic gift for the edification of the local church as revealed in First Corinthians 12–14. Pentecostal/ Charismatic. For another short study on this subject, see also, Robert E. Tourville, **Manifestations of the Spirit,** House of Bon Giovanni, 1985.

MALLONE, GEORGE. **Those Controversial Gifts.** Chicago: Inter-Varsity Press, 1971.

This work is a reaction to the book, **The Charismatics,** by John MacArthur. Mallone felt that MacArthur was extremely unfair in his study on the Gifts of the Spirit and Charismatics. Mallone is an evangelical open to all the gifts of the Holy Spirit for today. He does not write from a classical pentecostal point of view.

MARTIN, RALPH. **The Spirit and the Congregation.** Grand Rapids: Wm. B. Eerdmans Publishing Co., 1986.

This work on First Corinthians 12–15 is contemporary in its approach to the study of the church, worship and the charismatic phenomenon. Many issues are still left unanswered, but this is a good book on an important subject.

FIRST CORINTHIANS 13

EDWARDS, JONATHAN. **Charity and Its Fruits.** London: Banner of Truth Trust, 1969.

Even though this work on First Corinthians 13 was first published in 1852, it is a classic worthy of careful consideration. Edwards shows how Christian love is to be manifested in the heart and life of the believer. For a shorter classic, see also, Henry Drummond, **The Greatest Thing in the World.** Fleming H. Revell Co., n.d.

FINNEY, CHARLES. **Attributes of Love.** Grand Rapids: Kregel Publications, 1966.

Finney was a vibrant preacher and author. This study on this important chapter of the Bible will prove helpful and stimulating. Arminian. See also, William Scroggie, **Love Life: I Corinthians 13,** Kregel Publications, 1979.

JONES, JOHN DANIEL. **The Greatest of These: An Exposition of First Corinthians 13.** London: Hodder and Stoughton, 1925.

These are some of the finest expository sermons on First Corinthians 13 in print today. They are both practical and inspirational. This work is now published by Klock and Klock Christian Publishers.

FIRST CORINTHIANS 15

BROWN, JOHN. **The Resurrection of Life: An Exposition of First Corinthians, XV, With a Discourse on Our Lord's Resurrection.** Minneapolis: Klock and Klock Christian Publishers, 1979.

John Brown was a most note-worthy Scottish minister of his day. This work is a thorough, expository, and practical exposition of First Corinthians 15. In addition, it contains some helpful footnotes.

CANDLISH, ROBERT SMITH. **Life in a Risen Saviour.** Minneapolis: Klock and Klock Christian Publishers, 1977.

This practical work contains some excellent sermons on First Corinthians 15 by an outstanding preacher. Candlish knew how to expose a text and apply the Truth to ones everyday living.

SECOND CORINTHIANS

BARRETT, CHARLES KINGSLEY. **A Commentary on the Second Epistle to the Corinthians.** Harper New Testament Commentaries. New York: Harper and Row, 1968.

Barrett's exegetical commentary on Second Corinthians is just as helpful as his work on First Corinthians. Once again, watch out for his liberal theology.

HODGE, CHARLES. **An Exposition of the Second Epistle to the Corinthians.** Grand Rapids: Baker Book House, 1980.

Galatians

Even though this commentary was written over 100 years ago, this work by Hodge is still valuable. This is a doctrinal and expositional study on Second Corinthians. Calvinistic.

HUGHES, PHILIP EDGCOMBE. **Paul's Second Epistle to the Corinthians.** New International Commentary on the New Testament. Grand Rapids: Wm. B. Eerdmans Publishing Co., 1962.

The two strong features of this conservative commentary are, the breadth of scholarship, and its theological contribution from several sources. This recent commentary is one of the best works on Second Corinthians in modern print.

MOULE, HANDLEY CARR GLYN. **The Second Epistle to the Corinthians.** Grand Rapids: Zondervan Publishing House, 1962.

Try not to get this writer confused with Charles Francis Digby Moule. This work on Second Corinthians by Handley Moule is an admirable commentary. It is a translation, paraphrase and a forceful exposition all in one volume with an inclusion of footnotes.

REDPATH, ALAN. **Blessings Out of Buffetings.** Westwood, N. J.: Fleming H. Revell Co., 1965.

In this homiletical study, Redpath has given us some excellent devotional and evangelistic messages on second Corinthians. This is not a verse-by-verse commentary.

ROBERTSON, ARCHIBALD THOMAS. **The Glory of the Ministry.** Grand Rapids: Baker Book House, 1967.

This work deals with Paul's discourse on preaching from Second Corinthians 2:12 to 6:10. It is one of the best works available on these important passages of Scripture. Expository and exegetical.

GALATIANS

BROWN, JOHN. **An Exposition of the Epistle of Paul the Apostle to the Galatians.** Minneapolis:Klock and Klock Christian Publishers, 1979.

In this Puritan work, Brown delivers a powerful exposition

on the Book of Galatians. This commentary is loaded with sermonic material. Expository.

HENDRICKSEN, WILLIAM. **Exposition of Galatians.** New Testament Commentary. Grand Rapids: Baker Book House, 1968.

Hendricksen always writes a thorough commentary. This work is conservative, practical, up-to-date and exegetical in its approach to Galatians. It is a good solid work from the Reformed tradition.

HOGG, C. F. AND WILLIAM EDWY VINE. **The Epistle to the Galatians.** London: Pickering and Inglis, 1959.

An important doctrinal commentary dealing with some practical aspects of Galatians. This work contains helpful exegetical studies. For a more extensive doctrinal commentary, see also, Martin Luther, **Commentary on Galatians,** Kregel Publications, 1978.

LIGHTFOOT, JOSEPH BARBER. **The Epistle of St. Paul to the Galatians.** Grand Rapids: Zondervan Publishing House, 1966.

Even though this exegetical commentary was first published in 1865, it has never lost its appeal and value for New Testament study. While a knowledge of some Greek would be helpful, it will still be of great value to the average minister. For another similar work, see also, Frederick F. Bruce, **Galatians,** New International Greek Testament Commentary, Wm. B. Eerdmans Publishing Co., 1986.

MOULE, HANDLEY CARR GLYN. **The Second Epistle to the Corinthians.** Grand Rapids: Zondervan Publishing House, 1962.

Readers will discover a lot of homiletic extracts from this volume. The author gives a careful translation of the text, with a free paraphrase. This is an extremely practical exposition. For another good devotional commentary, see also, Lehman Strauss, **Devotional Studies in Galatians and Ephesians,** Loizeaux Brothers, 1957.

RAMSEY, WILLIAM MITCHELL. **A Historical Commentary on St. Paul's Epistle to the Galatians.** Minneapolis: Klock and Klock Christian Publishers, 1978.

In this classic volume, Ramsey deals with the history of religion, society, thought, manners, and education during the time of the Apostle Paul. Expository. This book can also be purchased in paperback from Baker Book House.

RIDDERBOS, HERMAN NICHOLAS. **The Epistle of Paul to the Churches of Galatia.** The New International Commentary on the New Testament. Grand Rapids: Wm. B. Eerdmans Publishing Co., 1953.

Bible students and pastors will want to purchase this work. Ridderbos has gained an excellent theological grasp of Paul's argument. He is not afraid to tackle the controversial problems of the Galatian letter. Expository.

STOTT, JOHN ROBERT WALMSEY. **The Message of Galatians.** London: Inter-Varsity Press, 1968.

Stott's work is not a verse-by-verse commentary. The book is valuable from a homiletical standpoint. Stott is an excellent expository preacher, and this work will aid the minister in preparing messages on the Book of Galatians.

TENNEY, MERRILL CHAPIN. **Galatians: The Character of Christian Liberty.** Grand Rapids: Wm. B. Eerdmans Publishing Co., 1954.

This work is not meant to be a verse-by-verse commentary. Instead, the author provides the reader with a concise and comprehensive analysis of Galatians by employing all the various methods of Bible Study. For some excellent notes on Galatians 1–3, see, John H. Skilton, **Machen's Notes on Galatians,** Presbyterian and Reformed Publishing Co., 1972.

THE FRUIT OF THE SPIRIT

BARCLAY, WILLIAM. **Flesh and Spirit: An Examination of Galatians 5:19–23.** Nashville: Abingdon Press, 1962.

Barclay has drawn extensively from his vast knowledge of history and language in this important study of "the fruit of the Spirit," and "the works of the flesh." This work is also available in paperback from Baker Book House.

BICKET, ZENAS J. **Walking in the Spirit.** Springfield, MO: Gospel Publishing House, 1977.

Dr. Bicket demonstrates that fruit bearing is extremely important in determining spirituality. This work gives a clear and practical exposition of "the fruit of the Spirit." Pentecostal/Charismatic.

DRESCHER, JOHN M. **Spirit Fruit.** Scottsdale, PA: Herald Press, 1975.

This is one of the most thorough expositions on Galatians 5:22–23 in print today. Drescher will aid any minister in preparing a series of messages on "the fruit of the Spirit." Arminian.

EPHESIANS

BRUCE, FREDERICK FYVIE. **Ephesians, Colossians and Philemon.** The New International Commentary on the New Testament. Grand Rapids: Wm. B. Eerdmans Publishing Co., 1986.

Please do not confuse this updated, revised and expanded volume with the older work by Simpson and Bruce. This book by Bruce easily replaces the other commentary in this series. For another good recent work, see also, Francis Foulkes, **The Epistle of Paul to the Ephesians,** Tyndale New Testament Commentaries, Wm. B. Eerdmans Publishing Co., 1963.

HENDRICKSEN, WILLIAM. **Exposition of Ephesians.** New Testament Commentary. Grand Rapids: Baker Book House, 1968.

This is one of the best modern commentaries on Ephesians. The author combines doctrine, exegesis and traces the themes and arguments of this Epistle. In addition, Hendricksen makes an excellent application of the text. For an older doctrinal commentary, see, Charles Hodge, **Commentary on the Epistle to the Ephesians,** Baker Book House, 1966.

MACARTHUR, JOHN, JR. **Ephesians: The MacArthur New Testament Commentary.** Chicago: Moody Press, 1986.

In this recent homiletical commentary, MacArthur gives the

minister some rich illustrations with careful exposition and practical application of the text. For a more extensive homiletical commentary, see, David Martyn Lloyd-Jones, **Ephesians,** 8 vols., Baker Book House, 1972–1984.

PATTISON, R. E. AND H. C. G. MOULE. **Exposition of Ephesians: Lessons in Grace and Godliness.** Minneapolis: Klock and Klock Christian Publishers, 1980.

In this volume, one will find Pattison's **Commentary on Ephesians** and Moule's **Expository Messages on Ephesians.** Even though both of these are older works, they are valuable for Bible students today. For another good work by Moule, see also, H. C. G. Moule, **Ephesian Studies: Lessons in Faith and Walk,** Zondervan Publishing House, n. d.

PAXSON, RUTH. **The Wealth, Walk and Warfare of the Christian.** Westwood, N. J.: Fleming H. Revell Co., 1939.

These devotional expositions on Ephesians are very helpful. Paxson was an outstanding writer of various practical books. For another good devotional work on Ephesians, see also, Watchman Nee, **Sit, Walk, Stand,** Christian Literature Crusade, 1963.

STOTT, JOHN ROBERT WALMSEY. **God's New Society: The Message of Ephesians.** The Bible Speaks Today. Downers Grove, IL: Inter-Varsity Press, 1979.

In this work, Dr. Stott delivers some excellent expository messages. For those preparing to preach a series of messages on Ephesians, Stott is deserving of your attention.

WESTCOTT, BROOKE FOSS. **Saint Paul's Epistle to the Ephesians.** Grand Rapids: Baker Book House, 1979.

For those who want to do some serious exegetical study on Ephesians, Westcott's commentary is a must. This work is also available in hardback from Klock and Klock Christian Publishers. For a more recent exegetical commentary with the Greek text, see also, Joseph A. Robinson, **Commentary on Ephesians,** Kregel Publications, 1979. Can be used without a knowledge of the Greek language.

EPHESIANS 6

GURNALL, WILLIAM. **The Christian in Complete Armor.**
London: Banner of Truth Trust, 1964.
For an excellent detailed study of the Christian armor passage in Ephesian 6, Gurnall's exposition is extremely helpful. This classic work was first published in 1655. For a more up-to-date exposition, see David Martyn Lloyd-Jones, **The Christian Warfare: An Exposition of Ephesians 6:10 to 13,** Baker Book House, 1977.

PHILIPPIANS

BOICE, JAMES MONTGOMERY. **Philippians: An Expositional Commentary.** Zondervan Publishing House, 1971.
In this excellent homiletical commentary, Dr. Boice, displays competent scholarship in an up-to-date style. Boice is an outstanding expository preacher. For another good example of expository preaching on this Epistle, see also, Guy H. King, **Joy Way,** Christian Literature Crusade, 1954.

EADIE, JOHN. **A Commentary on the Greek Text of the Epistle of Paul to the Philippians.** Minneapolis: James and Klock Publishing Co., 1977.
This classic commentary on Philippians was first published in 1859. It was written for the minister that would like to do some advanced study on this Epistle. For another excellent classic commentary with the Greek text, see also, J. B. Lightfoot, **St. Paul's Epistle to the Philippians,** Hendrickson Publishers, 1986. Sometimes you will have to read around the Greek text, but one can still use these two works without a minimal loss.

HENDRICKSEN, WILLIAM. **A Commentary on the Epistle to the Philippians.** New Testament Commentary. Grand Rapids: Baker Book House, 1962.
This is one of the better modern works on this Epistle. Hendricksen always has a good blend of technical, practical, and pastoral help in his commentaries. For another modern helpful

commentary, see also, **The Epistles of Paul to the Philippians and to Philemon,** The New International Commentary on the New Testament, Wm. B. Eerdmans Publishing Co., 1967.

JOHNSTONE, ROBERT. **Lectures on the Epistle to the Philippians.** Minneapolis: Klock and Klock Christian Publishers, 1977.

In this classic reprint, ministers will find a lot of helpful information. This work is a valuable, practical and homiletical commentary. First published in 1875. For another helpful older work, see also, Marvin C. Vincent, **A Critical and Exegetical Commentary on the Epistles to the Philippians and to Philemon,** International Critical Commentary, Charles Scribner's Sons, 1897.

MEYER, FREDERICK BROTHERTON. **Devotional Commentary on Philippians.** Grand Rapids: Kregel Publications, 1978.

This verse-by-verse devotional commentary is inspirational and challenging. It is a series of textual sermons that exhibit a combination of thorough scholarship and practical application. For a similar devotional commentary, see also, J. H. Jowett, **The High Calling,** Fleming H. Revell Co., 1909.

MOULE, HANDLEY CARR GLYN. **Philippian Studies: Lessons in Faith and Love.** Grand Rapids: Zondervan Publishing House, n. d.

This is a rewarding and devotional commentary. Moule wrote another work on Philippians in another series of commentaries, but this one is far more superior. For another excellent devotional work, see also, Lehman Strauss, **Devotional Studies in Philippians,** Loizeaux Brothers, 1970.

ROBERTSON, ARCHIBALD THOMAS. **Paul's Joy in Christ: Studies in Philippians.** Revised and edited by W. C. Strickland. Nashville: Broadman Press, 1959.

These devotional studies in Philippians are helpful to the expositor. It treats Paul's letter paragraph-by-paragraph rather than a verse-by-verse exposition.

VAUGHAN, CHARLES JOHN. **Epistle to the Philippians.** Minneapolis: Klock and Klock Christian Publishers, 1979.

Vaughan's expository messages on this Epistle is considered

a classic. Ministers will welcome this valuable reprint for help in preparing a series of sermons on the Book of Philippians. For another helpful reprint of an older work, see also, John Hutchinson, **An Exposition of Paul's Epistle to the Philippians,** Klock and Klock Christian Publishers, 1979.

COLOSSIANS

DAILLE, JEAN. **Exposition of Colossians.** Minneapolis: Klock and Klock Christian Publishers, 1979.

Daille's work has been eagerly sought after for years by students of the Bible. This valuable evangelical work has now been reprinted. It contains 698 pages. Calvinistic. For another valuable reprint, see also, Brooke F. Westcott, **The Epistle to the Colossians,** Klock and Klock Christian Publishers, 1979. This work can also be purchased in paperback from Baker Book House.

EADIE, JOHN. **Colossians.** Minneapolis: Klock and Klock Christian Publishers, 1979.

This work is valuable for its exposition and its study of the original text. A helpful, classic reprint. For another good classic reprint, see also, Joseph B. Lightfoot, **St. Paul's Epistle to the Colossians and Philemon,** Hendrickson Publishers, 1986.

GUTHRIE, THOMAS. **Christ and The Inheritance of the Saints.** Grand Rapids: Zondervan Publishing House, n. d.

In this study on Colossians 1:12–20, Guthrie delivers some excellent expository thoughts. This work was published in 1858, but it is still helpful for the expositor.

HENDRICKSEN, WILLIAM. **Exposition of Colossians and Philemon.** New Testament Commentary. Grand Rapids: Baker Book House, 1964.

Included in this commentary is a valuable introduction, the author's own translation, a verse-by-verse exposition, synthesis and a summary of thought for organization. In addition, there are some critical notes for special study. For another good modern commentary, see also, Homer A. Kent. **Trea-**

sures of Wisdom: Studies in Colossians and Philemon, Baker Book House, 1978.

KING, GUY HOPE. **Crossing the Border: An Expositional Study of Colossians.** Fort Washington, PA: Christian Literature Crusade, 1969.

King has been overlooked by a lot of ministers. All of his books are valuable from a homiletical standpoint. This devotional work on Colossians will be helpful to the Bible student and minister. For another good devotional exposition, see also, Henry A. Ironside, **Lectures on the Epistle to the Colossians,** Loizeaux Brothers, 1955.

MOULE, HANDLEY CARR GLYN. **Colossians and Philemon Studies: Lessons in Faith and Holiness.** Grand Rapids: Zondervan Publishing House, n.d.

Moule's commentary on the English text was first published in 1877. It is a valuable, practical exposition. His other work on Colossians and Philemon can be purchased in paperback from Kregel Publications. For another good older work on Colossians, see also, Alexander Maclaren, **Colossians,** The Expositor's Bible, Wm. B. Eerdmans Publishing Co., 1968.

NICHOLSON, WILLIAM RUFUS. **Colossians: Oneness with Christ.** Grand Rapids: Kregel Publications, 1973.

Here are some valuable expository lectures on the Book of Colossians. The author gives the reader a combination of outstanding scholarship and an excellent devotional tone. Highly regarded by Dr. Wilber M. Smith.

ROBERTSON, ARCHIBALD THOMAS. **Paul and the Intellectuals: The Epistle to the Colossians.** Revised and edited by W. C. Strickland. Nashville: Broadman Press, 1959.

This outstanding commentary began as the Stone Lectures for 1926. Robertson clearly reveals how Paul faced the intellectual leaders of his day. A helpful verse-by-verse exposition. For helpful outline studies, see also, William Henry Griffith Thomas, **Studies in Colossians and Philemon,** Baker Book House, 1973.

I AND II THESSALONIANS

HENDRIKSEN, WILLIAM. **Exposition of I and II Thessalonians.** New Testament Commentary. Grand Rapids: Baker Book House, 1964.

This commentary will be a welcome edition to every minister's library. It is especially valuable for its recent scholarship. Hendricksen is always practical. Amillennial.

HIEBERT, DAVID EDMOND. **The Thessalonian Epistles.** Chicago: Moody Press, 1971.

Hiebert offers the student and minister comprehensive exegesis and detailed outlines of both epistles. In addition, he provides a comparison of other authors and provides some valuable background information on the city and culture of the Thessalonian Church. Premillennial. For another premillennial commentary, see also, John F. Walvoord, **The Thessalonian Epistles,** Dunham Publishing Company, 1967.

HOGG, CHARLES FREDERICK AND WILLIAM EDWY VINE. **The Epistles to the Thessalonians.** Fincastle, VA: Scripture Truth Book Company, 1959.

In this exposition, Hogg and Vine present some excellent material that is both exegetical and expository. This work is loaded with helpful information on these epistles. Premillennial.

MILLIGAN, GEORGE. **St. Paul's Epistles to the Thessalonians.** Minneapolis: Klock and Klock Christian Publishers, 1980.

At one time, this excellent work was difficult to find. Milligan was an outstanding New Testament writer. This exegetical work includes a good summary on the person of the Antichrist. Amillennial. For another good exegetical older work, see also, John Eadie, **Commentary on the Epistle to the Thessalonians,** James and Klock Publishing Co., 1977.

MORRIS, LEON. **The First and Second Epistle to the Thessalonians.** New International Commentary on the New Testament. Grand Rapids: Wm. B. Eerdmans Publishing co., 1976.

This modern commentary abounds with fresh exegetical

studies and relates the message to the reader's personal faith. A good balanced commentary. Amillennial.

OCKENGA, HAROLD JOHN. **The Church in God.** Westwood, N. J.: Fleming H. Revell Co., 1956.

Every minister can benefit from studying Ockenga's exository sermons. Ockenga was an excellent expository preacher. This volume on Thessalonians is helpful. Premillennial.

PASTORAL EPISTLES

FAIRBAIRN, PATRICK. **Pastoral Epistles.** Minneapolis: James and Klock Publishing Co., 1976.

Fairbairn writes with a pastor's heart. This classic exposition will always be a helpful guide to the Pastoral Epistles. Even though this reprint is based on the 1874 edition, it is still valuable today. Conservative.

GUTHRIE, DONALD. **The Pastoral Epistles.** Tyndale New Testament Commentaries. Grand Rapids: Wm. B. Eerdmans Publishing Co., 1957.

In this critical and exegetical work, the average minister will be amazed at the amount of recent, helpful information. This is one of the more valuable works in this series of commentaries. For a more scholarly approach, see, Edmund K. Simpson, **The Pastoral Epistles,** Tyndale Press, 1954.

HENDRICKSEN, WILLIAM. **Exposition of the Pastoral Epistles.** New Testament Commentary. Grand Rapids: Baker Book House, 1968.

Hendricksen's work on the Pastoral Epistles is one of the best modern commentaries today. He defends the Pauline authorship and provides an exegetical and practical study of the text. Conservative.

KELLY, JOHN NORMAN DAVIDSON. **The Pastoral Epistles.** Harper's New Testament Commentaries. New York: Harper and Row Publishers, 1963.

Of all the commentaries in this series, Kelly is one of the more conservative writers. This exegetical commentary is extensive in scope and ably defends the Pauline authorship.

KENT, HOMER AUSTIN, JR. **The Pastoral Epistles: Studies in I and II Timothy and Titus.** Chicago: Moody Press, 1958.

This conservative writer presents a well-balanced commentary on the Pastoral Epistles. Some writers have difficulty bringing the exegetical and practical together in one volume but Kent has both.

VINE, WILLIAM EDWY. **The Epistles to Timothy and Titus: Faith and Conduct.** Grand Rapids: Zondervan Publishing House, 1965.

Vine's satisfying exposition on the Pastoral Epistles is written in a practical manner. And yet Vine shows good exegetical insight throughout this commentary. Conservative.

FIRST TIMOTHY

HIEBERT, DAVID EDMOND. **First Timothy.** Chicago: Moody Press, 1957.

Hiebert is an oustanding New Testament writer. This work on First Timothy is balanced, exegetical and modern in its approach to this important epistle. For a good homiletical commentary, see, Guy H. King, **A Leader Led: A Devotional Study of I Timothy,** Marshall, Morgan and Scott, 1953.

LIDDON, HENRY PARRY. **Explanatory Analysis of St. Paul's First Epistle to Timothy.** Minneapolis: Klock and Klock Christian Publishers, 1978.

At one time, this work by Liddon was difficult to find. It has now been reprinted. Even though it is based on the Greek text, a minister without a knowledge of the original language can still profit from this book. For a more extensive, devotional work, see, Alfred Rowland, **Studies in I Timothy,** Klock and Klock Christian Publishers, 1978.

SECOND TIMOTHY

HIEBERT, DAVID EDMOND. **Second Timothy.** Chicago: Moody Press, 1958.

Another excellent volume from the pen of Hiebert. This conservative work deals with every need in the study of Paul's First Epistle to Timothy. Practical.

MOULE, HANDLEY CARR GLYN. **Studies in II Timothy.** Grand Rapids: Kregel Publications, 1977.

Even though this brief commentary was first published in 1905, it is still a devotional classic worth consulting. For another good devotional and homiletical commentary, see also, Guy H. King, **To My Son: An Expositional Study of II Timothy,** Marshall, Morgan and Scott, 1953.

TITUS

HIEBERT, DAVID EDMOND. **Titus and Philemon.** Chicago: Moody Press, 1957.

Once again, Hiebert gives a balanced approach to Paul's Epistles. This commentary is both exegetical and practical. It is a careful study in every detail. Conservative.

TAYLOR, THOMAS. **Exposition of Titus.** Minneapolis: Klock and Klock Christian Publishers, 1980.

While this classic reprint is extensive, and old, it will still be helpful to the Bible student and minister. This work contains 665 pages. Puritan and Calvinistic.

PHILEMON

COX, SAMUEL AND A. H. DRYSDALE. **The Epistle to Philemon.** Minneapolis: Klock and Klock Christian Publishers, 1979.

Cox and Drysdale's works on Philemon have now been combined into one volume by this publisher. Both volumes are good examples of Bible exposition. The comments in these books are extremely helpful.

SCROGGIE, WILLIAM GRAHAM. **Studies in Philemon.** Grand Rapids: Kregel Publications, 1977.

A worthy devotional and expositional study on Philemon by

a gifted writer. This is a rewarding in-depth study of a very neglected book of the Bible. Conservative. (Please note: For other commentaries on Philemon see under Colossians and the Prison Epistles of Paul.)

GENERAL EPISTLES

HIEBERT, DAVID EDMOND. **An Introduction to the Non-Pauline Epistles.** Chicago: Moody Press, 1962.
Easily one of the most up-to-date, conservative works on the General Epistles. Before doing any serious study on background and content of these books of the Bible, one will want to consult Hiebert over and over again. For a smaller conservative work, see, Charles R. Erdman, **The General Epistles,** Westminster Press, 1918.

HEBREWS

BROWN, JOHN. **An Exposition of the Epistle of the Apostle Paul to the Hebrews.** London: Banner of Truth Trust, reprint.
This is a classic reprint of the 1862 edition. In this rewarding exposition, Brown stays close to the original text and makes a practical application to the life of the believer. For another good older work, see also, Alexander B. Bruce, **The Epistle to the Hebrews: The First Apology for Christianity; an Exegetical Study,** Klock and Klock Christian Publishers, 1980.
BRUCE, FREDERICK FYVIE. **The Epistle to the Hebrews.** New International Commentary on the New Testament. Grand Rapids: Wm. B. Eerdmans Publishing Co., 1964.
Dr. Bruce has developed a thorough exegetical commentary based upon the original text. Bruce's use of extensive footnotes reflects mature scholarship. For another useful work, see also, William R. Newell, **Hebrews, Verse by Verse,** Moody Press, 1947.
DELITZSCH, FRANZ JULIUS. **Commentary on the Epis-**

tle to the Hebrews. 2 vols. Minneapolis: Klock and Klock Christian Publishers, 1978.

In this classic reprint, Delitzsch follows the Greek text carefully in dealing with critical problems in Hebrews. An excellent defense of the doctrine of the atonement. The author demonstrates an excellent grasp of the Hebrew and Greek languages. For another good older work on the Greek text, see also, Brooke F. Westcott, **The Epistle to the Hebrews,** Wm. B. Eerdmans Publishing Co., reprint.

EDWARDS, THOMAS CHARLES. **The Epistle to the Hebrews.** Minneapolis: Klock and Klock Christian Publishers, 1978.

This expositional commentary is based upon the English text. Edwards was a careful writer on the New Testament. He blends careful exposition and application. For the same commentary, see also, Thomas C. Edwards, **The Epistle to the Hebrews,** The Expositor's Bible, Wm. B. Eerdmans Publishing Co., 1968.

HUGHES, PHILLIP EDGCOMBE. **A Commentary on the Epistle to the Hebrews.** Grand Rapids: Wm. B. Eerdmans Publishing Co., 1984.

Of all the commentaries on Hebrews, this is one of the best and most up-to-date for a conservative writer. This 625 page work is almost essential for every minister's library.

MACARTHUR, JOHN F. JR. **The MacArthur New Testament Commentary: Hebrews,** Chicago: Moody Press, 1985.

For a good homiletical commentary, MacArthur is very helpful. This recent exposition is of value for ideas on a series of sermons from Hebrews. For a good older work, see also, William H. G. Thomas, **Hebrews: A Devotional Commentary,** Wm. B. Eerdmans Publishing Co., 1962.

MURRAY, ANDREW. **The Holiest of All.** New York: Fleming H. Revell Co., 1965.

The best devotional and practical commentary on the book of Hebrews is this one by Murray. For another brief devotional work, see also, Frederick B. Meyer, **The Way Into the Holiest,** Christian Literature Crusade, 1968.

MILLIGAN, GEORGE. **The Theology of the Epistle to the**

Hebrews, With a Critical Introduction. Minneapolis: Klock and Klock Christian Publishers, 1978.

Even though this classic work was first published in 1899, it is still helpful today. This significant reprint is for the serious student. For another significant reprint, see also, Adolph Saphir, **The Epistle to the Hebrews,** Kregel Publications, 1983.

MORGAN, GEORGE CAMPBELL. **God's Last Word to Man.** New York: Fleming H. Revell Co., 1936.

This is not a verse-by-verse commentary. It is a helpful collection of expositions on certain verses of the Book of Hebrews. Now available in paperback from Baker Book House. For another good older work in paperback, see also, John Owen, **Hebrews: The Epistle of Warning,** Kregel Publications, 1968.

HEBREWS 11

BULLINGER, ETHELBERT WILLIAM. **Great Cloud of Witnesses in Hebrews Eleven.** Grand Rapids: Kregel Publications, 1979.

A complete exposition of Hebrews chapter 11 dealing with the heroes of faith. Bullinger has some extremes in dispensational theology, but this work is still very helpful.

MORGAN, GEORGE CAMPBELL. **The Triumphs of Faith.** London: Pickering and Inglis LTD., 1975.

This exposition of Hebrews 11 is an outstanding example of good expository preaching. Here are seventeen inspiring chapters on faith from an outstanding Bible teacher and preacher. This work is now available in paperback from Baker Book House.

HEBREWS 12

SAUER, ERICH ERNST. **In the Arena.** Grand Rapids: Wm. B. Eerdmans Publishing Co., 1955.

Sauer was an outstanding writer on several subjects. This

work on Hebrews 12 is extremely helpful. It abounds with practical application to the Christian life. Conservative.

JAMES

HIEBERT, DAVID EDMOND. **The Epistle of James: Tests of a Living Faith.** Chicago: Moody Press, 1979.

Hiebert delivers another high quality exposition and up-to-date commentary. He thoroughly explains the intention of the author in writing this Epistle. Evangelical and practical. For another excellent recent work, see also, Charles Leslie Mitton, **The Epistle of James,** Wm. B. Eerdmans Publishing Co., 1966.

JOHNSTONE, ROBERT. **Lectures, Exegetical and Practical, on the Epistle of James.** Minneapolis: Klock and Klock Christian Publishers, 1978.

The title of this book says it all. Johnstone brings together a balanced exposition, both practical and exegetical on this important epistle. Very helpful and a classic reprint of the 1871 edition. For another good classic work, but with the Greek text, see also, Joseph B. Mayor, **The Epistle of St. James,** Klock and Klock Christian Publishers, 1977.

MANTON, THOMAS. **An Exposition of the Epistle of James.** London: Banner of Truth Trust, n. d.

Manton's devotional commentary on James is a classic. It is somewhat wordy, but it is full of application and practical help. Good expository preaching from a well-known Puritan writer.

ROBERTSON, ARCHIBALD THOMAS. **Studies in the Epistle of James.** Revised and edited by Herber F. Peacock. Nashville: Broadman Press, 1959.

A very practical and helpful exposition on the Epistle of James. For another excellent, expositional study, see also, Guy H. King, **A Belief That Behaves,** Christian Literature Crusade, 1963.

ROSS, ALEXANDER. **The Epistle of James and John.** New International Commentary on the New Testament. Grand Rapids: Wm. B. Eerdmans Publishing Co., 1954.

A helpful work containing both the Epistle of James and the

Epistles of John. The author ably defends the Johannie author-ship of John's epistles. For a better work on James, see also, James B. Adamson, **The Epistle of James,** New International Commentary on the New Testament, Wm. B. Eerdmans Pub-lishing Co., 1976.

STIER, RUDOLF E. **Commentary on the Epistle of James.** Minneapolis: Klock and Klock Christian Publishers, 1979.

Some of Stier's theology cannot be accepted, but his com-mentary is helpful. This work is a series of expository mes-sages on the Epistle of James. For another helpful work, see also, Randolph V. G. Tasker, **The General Epistle of James,** Tyndale New Testament Commentaries, Wm. B. Eerdmans Publishing Co., 1960.

ZODHIATES, SPIROS. **The Behavior of Belief.** Grand Rapids: Wm. B. Eerdmans Publishing Co., 1970.

Easily the best, recent, homiletical commentary in print to-day. This extensive work on James is loaded with preaching material. For a smaller, homiletical commentary, see also, Lehman Strauss, **James Your Brother: Studies in the Epistle of James,** Loizeaux Brothers, 1956.

PETER'S EPISTLES

JOWETT, JOHN HENRY. **The Epistles of St. Peter.** Grand Rapids: Kregel Publications, 1970.

Jowett's work on these epistles is extremely helpful and practical. It is a series of devotional expositions from the pen of a gifted writer. This commentary is a reprint from the 1904 edition. For a more extensive devotional study on the epistles of Peter, see also, John Lillie, **Lectures on First and Second Peter,** Klock and Klock Christian Publishers, 1978.

FIRST PETER

BROWN, JOHN. **Expository Discourses in the First Epistle of the Apostle Peter.** 3 vols. Marshalltown Del.: National Foundation for Christian Education, n. d.

Even though this work was first published in 1848, it is an expositional classic. This is a wordy, phrase-by-phrase commentary. Now available from Banner of Truth Trust in 2 volumes.

HIEBERT, DAVID EDMOND. **First Peter: An Expositional Commentary.** Chicago: Moody Press, 1985.

Hiebert is a warm Arminian/Mennonite writer. All of his works are worth purchasing for the minister's library. Here is another balanced, detailed and exegetical commentary on the Epistle of First Peter. For another good recent commentary, see also, Alan M. Stibbs, **The First Epistle of Peter.** Tyndale New Testament Commentaries. Wm. B. Eerdmans Publishing Co., 1960.

LEIGHTON, ROBERT. **First Peter.** Grand Rapids: Kregel Publications, 1974.

This valuable work is unparalleled even though it was published in 1831. Leighton gives the reader a balance of thorough exposition with a warm devotional application. For another older work, see also, Fenton J. A. Hort and Sir Arthur Fenton Hort, **Expository and Exegetical Studies,** Klock and Klock Christian Publishers, 1978. This work also includes studies on the Apocalypse, James, Romans, Ephesians and Mark.

MEYER, FREDERICK BROTHERTON. **Tried By Fire: Expositions of the First Epistle of Peter.** Fort Washington, PA: Christian Literature Crusade, 1970.

Meyer's work on First Peter has now been reprinted from the 1890 edition. Like most of this gifted writer's commentaries, there is always a strong devotional emphasis. Practical. For an outlined commentary on the Epistles of Peter, see comments under **Bible Characters from the Gospels and Peter,** by William H. G. Thomas.

SELWYN, EDWARD GORDON. **First Epistle of St. Peter.** London: Macmillan Co., 1961.

The major value of this work lies in its recent scholarship and exegetical thoroughness. This commentary is based on the Greek text, but it is not overly technical. Now available in paperback from Baker Book House.

SECOND PETER

GREEN, EDWARD MICHAEL BANKS. **Second Epistle General of Peter and the General Epistle of Jude.** Tyndale New Testament Commentary. Grand Rapids: Wm. B. Eerdmans Publishing Co., 1968.

Green's work on Second Peter is one of the better volumes in this series of commentaries. This commentary is both exegetical and practical. For a good homiletical commentary on Second Peter, see also, D. Martyn Lloyd-Jones, **Expository Sermons on 2nd. Peter,** Banner of Truth Trust, n. d.

JOHN'S EPISTLES

CANDLISH, ROBERT SMITH. **First Epistle of John.** Grand Rapids: Kregel Publications, 1979.

This work by Candlish has long been the classic work on the First Epistle of John. It is clear, concise and practical. For another excellent classic, see also, George G. Findlay, **Fellowship in the Life Eternal: An Exposition of the Epistles of John.** Minneapolis: James and Klock Publishing Co., 1977.

LAW, ROBERT. **The Tests of Life. A Study of the First Epistle of John.** 3d ed. Grand Rapids: Baker Book House, 1968.

A valuable classic reprint that was hard to obtain for several years. This is a well-balanced exposition. For another older classic based on the Greek text, see also, Alfred Pummer, **The Epistles of St. John,** Baker Book House, 1980.

MARSHALL, I. HOWARD. **The Epistles of John,** The International Commentary on the New Testament. Grand Rapids: Wm. B. Eerdmans Publishing Co., 1978.

Marshall's commentary is valuable and helpful because of its recent scholarship. For another good exegetical work that is based on the Greek text, see also, Brooke F. Westcott, **The Epistles of St. John,** Wm. B. Eerdmans Publishing Co., 1966.

MORGAN, JAMES, AND SAMUEL COX. **The Epistles of**

John. Minneapolis: Klock and Klock Christian Publishers, 1979.

Now both of these author's works have been published in one volume. This outstanding work of exposition contains 612 pages. For another older exposition based on the Greek text, see also, John J. Lias, **The First Epistle of John,** Klock and Klock Christian Publishers, 1979.

STEDMAN, RAY C. **Expository Studies in I John: Life By the Son.** Waco, TX: Word Books, 1980.

Stedman's homiletical commentary is excellent. It is loaded with practical application. For another good work that will help the expositor, see also, Henry A. Ironside, **Addresses on the Epistles of John and an Exposition of Jude,** Loizeaux Brothers, 1954.

STOTT, JOHN ROBERT WALMSEY. **The Epistles of John.** Tyndale New Testament Commentaries. Grand Rapids: Wm. B. Eerdmans Publishing co., 1964.

Stott's commentaries and expository studies are extremely valuable. For another excellent, practical exposition, see also, Guy H. King, **The Fellowship,** Christian Literature Crusade, 1968.

VINE, WILLIAM EDWY. **The Epistles of John.** Grand Rapids: Zondervan Publishing House, reprint.

Even though this author had an excellent grasp of the Greek language, he always makes it clear enough for a novice to understand. Practical and helpful.

JUDE

CODER, S. MAXWELL. **Jude: The Acts of the Apostates.** Chicago: Moody Press, 1958.

Even though this commentary is brief, it is to the point and loaded with helpful information. For a more extensive and helpful commentary based on the original text, see also, George L. Lawlor, **Translation and Exposition of the Epistle of Jude,** Presbyterian and Reformed Publishing Co., 1972.

MANTON, THOMAS. **An Exposition of the Epistle of Jude.** London: Banner of Truth Trust, 1958.

Manton's work on Jude is a classic. This important Puritan commentary can now be purchased from Klock and Klock Christian Publishers. Expository.

REVELATION

BECKWORTH, ISBON THADDAEUS. **The Apocalypse of John.** Grand Rapids: Baker Book House, 1967.

A helpful exegetical commentary that is based on sound scholarship. Amillennial. For another good volume that is based on the Greek text, see also, Henry B. Swete, **Commentary on Revelation,** Kregel Publications, 1977. Amillennial.

SEISS, JOSEPH AUGUSTUS. **The Apocalypse.** Grand Rapids: Zondervan Publishing House, 1964.

In this classic commentary, Seiss gives an able exposition of the Book of Revelation. Premillennial. For another helpful expository work, see also, Wallie A. Criswell, **Expository Sermons on the Book of Revelation,** Zondervan Publishing House, 1961–66. Premillennial.

SMITH, JACOB BRUBAKER. **A Revelation of Jesus Christ.** Edited by J. Otis Yoder. Scottdale, Penn.: Herald Press, 1961.

This careful study is exegetical and practical. It is especially helpful from an Arminian and Premillennial viewpoint. For another helpful work, see also, William R. Newell, **The Book of Revelation,** Moody Press, 1935. Premillennial.

STRAUSS, LEHMAN. **The Book of Revelation.** Neptune, N. J.: Loizeaux Brothers, 1965.

If a minister wants to prepare a series of messages on Revelation, Strauss will be a helpful guide to follow. These expository messages are practical. Premillennial. For another older, helpful exposition, see also, Walter Scott, **Exposition of the Revelation of Jesus Christ,** Kregel Publications, 1979. Premillennial.

TATFORD, FREDERICK ALBERT. **The Revelation.** Minneapolis: Klock and Klock Christian Publishers, 1979.

A clear, sound, Premillennial introduction to the events of the Book of Revelation. For another good older work, see also, Fenton John Anthony Hort, **The Apocalypse of St. John, I–II.,** James and Klock Christian Publishers, 1976.

TENNEY, MERRILL CHAPIN. **Interpreting Revelation.** Grand Rapids: Wm. B. Eerdmans Publishing Co., 1968.

An important work on the Book of Revelation. This book is not a verse-by-verse commentary. Instead, it is a basic handbook setting forth the various methods of interpretation. Premillennial.

WALVOORD, JOHN FLIPSE. **The Revelation of Jesus Christ.** Chicago: Moody Press, 1966.

Walvoord is well-known for his prophetic insights. This work is one of his best. Premillennial. For another recent commentary, see also, Robert H. Mounce, **The Book of Revelation,** New International Commentary on the New Testament, Wm. B. Eerdmans Publishing Co., 1977.

THE SEVEN CHURCHES

BARCLAY, WILLIAM. **Letters to the Seven Churches.** New York: Abingdon Press, 1958.

Barclay's historical work on the Seven Churches is excellent. For another excellent historical study, see also, William M. Ramsey, **Letters to the Seven Churches of Asia,** Baker Book House, 1963.

MORGAN, GEORGE CAMPBELL. **The Letters of Our Lord: A First Century Message to Twentieth Century Christians.** London: Pickering and Inglis, 1961.

In this practical work, Morgan deals with the everyday conditions of church life. these expository studies are valuable and practical. This book is now available in paperback from Baker Book House. For a more exegetical work, see also, Richard C. Trench, **Commentary on the Epistle to the Seven Churches,** Klock and Klock Christian Publishers, 1978.

SEISS, JOSEPH AUGUSTUS. **Letters to the Seven Churches.** Grand Rapids: Baker Book House, 1956.

Even though this practical book was first published in 1889, it is still very helpful for expository values on the Seven Churches. For an excellent recent publication, see also, John R. W. Stott, **What Christ Thinks of the Church,** Wm. B. Eerdmans Publishing Co., 1958.

Books on Christian Theology

In recent years we have witnessed a resurgence of interest in Christian theology. It is fitting that a guide be written since there is a steady increase of new theological books coming off the presses weekly. What are some of the best books that will aid a minister in the content of Scripture and in the study of theology? This section will help to answer that question and deal with books about Christian doctrine as a whole.

The systematization of Christian theology is an important and logical task for the minister because the Bible is not systematically arranged. Theology is the complement of biblical exposition. A thorough knowledge of Christian doctrine gives the expositor a consistent and balanced view of God, man, salvation, and the world. The Apostle Paul was militant when it came to Christian theology. He condemned false teaching vigorously at Galatia (Galatians 1:6–9). False teaching will poison the soul of a person. In fact, it will destroy evangelism altogether. A proper knowledge of theology is at the very heart of a minister's preaching ministry. Unfortunately, too many preachers stop studying theology after college or seminary.

The books recommended in this section are framed with a view to acquainting the minister or Bible student with the tension points in theological circles today, in addition to providing a positive exposition of the biblical content in each case. In this section, the author will mention books from the Arminian and Calvinistic persuasions to keep a proper balance. One word of caution is in order at this point. In the field of Christian theology, there is a great danger of being deceived by some authors. The best safeguard to this problem is to search the Bible itself to test the teaching we receive from the various books on theology.

THEOLOGY

Baker's Dictionary of Theology. Edited by E. F. Harrison. Grand Rapids: Baker Book House, 1960.

Here is an excellent work containing 874 articles and over 7000 words on the subject of theology. This is a most valuable dictionary. Conservative. For another helpful work, see also Bernard L. Ramm, **A Handbook of Contemporary Theology,** Wm. B. Eerdmans Publishing Co., 1966.

SYSTEMATIC THEOLOGY

BERKHOF, LOUIS. **Systematic Theology.** 4th. rev. ed. Grand Rapids: Wm. B. Eerdmans Publishing Co., 1969.

A concise and compact compendium of Reformed theology by an excellent writer. This work is a classic on the study of systematic theology. Evangelical. For another good Reformed work, see also, Charles Hodge, **Systematic Theology,** 3 vols., Wm. B. Eerdmans Publishing Co., 1960.

BUSWELL, JAMES OLIVER, JR. **A Systematic Theology of the Christian Religion.** 2 vols. Grand Rapids: Zondervan Publishing House, 1962.

Buswell was a highly respected theologian. He was thoroughly acquainted with the original languages of the Bible. This conservative work is valuable from the Premillennial viewpoint.

FINNEY, CHARLES. **Finney's Lectures on Systematic Theology.** Edited by J. C. Fairchild. Grand Rapids: Wm. B. Eerdmans Publishing Co., 1969.

This work is valuable from an Arminian viewpoint of theology. Finney is the late president of Oberlin College and professor of Theology.

PEARLMAN, MYER. **Knowing the Doctrines of the Bible.** Springfield, MO.: Gospel Publishing House, 1937.

A basic, but helpful Arminian treatment of such subjects as God and Man, Sin and Salvation, Christ and the Church, and the Holy Spirit. Pentecostal/Charismatic. For another work on Bible doctrines, see also, William Evans, **The Great Doctrines of the Bible,** Rev. ed., Moody Press, 1964.

THIESSEN, HENRY CLARENCE. **Introductory Lectures in Systematic Theory.** Revised by Vernon D. Doerkson. Grand Rapids: Wm. B. Eerdmans Publishing Co., 1979.

An excellent work that discusses the essentials of theology

from the existence of God to the final state of man. Conservative and Premillennial.

STRONG, AUGUSTUS HOPKINS. **Systematic Theology.**
Valley Forge, Penn.: Judson Press, 1907.

Strong's work is best known for its general and overall coverage in the field of systematic theology. A good basic and helpful study. For another helpful, older work, see also, William G. T. Shedd, **Dogmatic Theology,** 3 vols., Klock and Klock Christian Publishers, 1979. Calvinistic.

WILEY, HENRY ORTON. **Christian Theology.** 3 vols.
Kansas City, MO: Beacon Hill Press, 1940.

This is one of the best recent works on Arminian and Wesleyan theology. It is both complete and thorough. Conservative and premillennial. For another Arminian work, see also, W. T. Purkiser, Richard S. Taylor, and Willard H. Taylor, **God, Man, and Salvation: A Biblical Theology,** Beacon Hill Press, 1977.

PENTECOSTAL/CHARISMATIC THEOLOGY

ELBERT, PAUL. **Essays on Apostolic Themes.** Peabody, MA: Hendrickson Publishers, 1986.

This work contains an important discussion of Pentecostal/Charismatic issues. Here is a summary of the dialogue that took place with Pentecostal/Charismatic and non-Pentecostal/Charismatic theologians.

ROBECK, CECIL M. JR. **Charismatic Experiences in History.** Peabody, MA: Hendrickson Publishers, 1986.

A series of essays by contributors of various backgrounds of faith and practice. This important book fills a substantial gap in dialogue about Pentecostal/Charismatic experience.

MODERN THEOLOGY

MACHEN, JOHN GRESHAM. **Christianity and Liberalism.** Grand Rapids: Wm. B. Eerdmans Publishing Co., 1923.

This admirable book presents a stringent defense of conservative Protestantism. It is one of the best discussions on the controversy between Christianity and Liberalism.

THE GODHEAD

BICKERSTETH, EDWARD HENRY. **The Trinity.** Grand Rapids: Kregel Publications, 1965.
Even though this work was first published in 1859, it is one of the most valuable treatments ever published on the Trinity. Conservative.

GOD THE FATHER

SPITTLER, RUSSELL P. **God the Father.** Springfield, MO.: Gospel Publishing House, 1984.
Spittler reveals God as a personal Father who loves individuals. A very basic study on the Nature of God. Devotional. For another good devotional work, see also, Lehman Strauss, **The First Person,** Loizeaux Brothers, 1967.

GOD THE HOLY SPIRIT

ERVIN, HOWARD M. **Conversion—Initiation and the Baptism in the Holy Spirit.** Peabody, MA: Hendrickson Publishers, 1986.
In this work, Ervin responds to James D. G. Dunn's work, **Baptism in the Holy Spirit.** The author refutes the hypothesis that the baptism in the Holy Spirit is a conversion-initiation event experienced by all believers. Pentecostal/Charismatic. For another Pentecostal/Charismatic series of studies, see also, **Conference on the Holy Spirit Digest,** Gwen Jones (comp.), Gospel Publishing House, 1983.
GORDON, ADONIRAM JUDSON. **The Ministry of the Spirit.** Minneapolis: Bethany Fellowship, 1965.

A deeply devotional examination on the work of the Holy Spirit. The interpretation is sound and balanced. Warmly evangelical. For another excellent devotional work, see also, James E. Cumming, **Through the Eternal Spirit,** Bethany Fellowship, 1965.

HORTON, STANLEY M. **What The Bible Says About The Holy Spirit.** Springfield, MO.: Gospel Publishing House, 1976.

This is a commentary on the Holy Spirit. Horton writes from an evangelical perspective with exegetical soundness. Pentecostal/Charismatic. For another work from a Pentecostal/ Charismatic viewpoint, see also, Dennis and Rita Bennett, **The Holy Spirit and You,** Logos International, 1971.

KUYPER, ABRAHAM. **The Work of the Holy Spirit.** Translated by Henri de Vries. Grand Rapids: Wm. B. Eerdmans Publishing Co., n. d.

An extremely well-written work on the study of the Holy Spirit. Kuyper's exegetical study is a Reformed classic. For another good classic, see also, George Smeaton, **The Doctrine of the Holy Spirit,** Banner of Truth Trust, 1958.

MURRAY, ANDREW. **The Spirit of Christ.** Fort Washington, Penn.: Christian Literature Crusade, 1964.

In this devotional work, Murray gives some excellent thoughts on the indwelling of the Holy Spirit in the believer and the church. For another good work, see also, Reuben A. Torrey, **The Holy Spirit: Who He Is and What He Does,** Fleming H. Revell Co., 1927.

OWEN, JOHN. **The Holy Spirit, His Gifts and Power.** Grand Rapids: Kregel Publications, 1960.

An outstanding one-volume study on the Person and Work of the Holy Spirit. This extensive work contains 356 pages. For another good older work, see also, Handley C. G. Moule, **Person and Work of the Holy Spirit, Kregel Publications, 1977.**

SIMPSON, ALBERT BENJAMIN. **The Holy Spirit or Power From on High.** 2 vols. Harrisburg, Penn.: Christian Publications, n. d.

In these practical volumes, Simpson delivers a series of sermons on the doctrine of the Holy Spirit in the Old and New Testaments. Arminian. For another good Arminian work, see also, Ralph M. Riggs, **The Spirit Himself,** Gospel Publishing House, 1968.

THOMAS, WILLIAM HENRY GRIFFITH. **The Holy Spirit of God.** Grand Rapids: Wm. B. Eerdmans Publishing Co., 1950.

This series of lectures on the Holy Spirit is one of the author's most valued and scholarly contributions. He discusses the Scriptural basis for the doctrines of the Holy Spirit. Evangelical. For another good older work, see also, G. Campbell Morgan, **The Spirit of God,** Hodder and Stoughton, 1907. This work is now available in paperback from Baker Book House.

ATTRIBUTES OF GOD

CHARNOCK, STEPHEN. **The Existence and Attributes of God.** Grand Rapids: Kregel Publications, n. d.

Charnock's classic study of sermons first appeared in 1797. This Puritan work is still helpful to the expositor. The author takes the doctrine of God and shows exhaustively how it affects the life of men. Calvinistic. This work is now available from Baker Book House in 2 volumes.

TOZER, AIDEN WILSON. **The Knowledge of the Holy.** New York: Harper and Brothers, 1961.

An outstanding exposition by an Arminian writer. Tozer's work on the attributes of God is one of his best writings. Practical and devotional.

PROVIDENCE OF GOD

FLAVEL, JOHN. **The Mystery of Providence.** London: Banner of Trùth Trust, 1963.

A helpful study dealing with God's oversight and control of everything that comes to pass and how this teaching can be of practical value to the individual believer. Calvinistic. For another helpful work, see also, **The Providence of God,** Studies in Dogmatics, Translated by Lewis Smedes, Wm. B. Eerdmans Publishing Co., 1952. Calvinistic.

SOVEREIGNTY OF GOD

BOICE, JAMES MONTGOMERY. **Foundations of the Christian Faith.** Vol. 1: **The Sovereign God.** Downer's Grove, IL: Inter-Varsity Press, 1978.

Boice discusses the person of God and the revelation of His will for mankind. A very practical and helpful work. Calvinistic.

PACKER, JAMES INNELL. **Evangelism and the Sovereignty of God.** London: Inter-Varsity Fellowship, 1961.

A helpful work showing the relationship between God's sovereignty and Christian evangelism. Packer is an excellent writer on various subjects. For an older classic work, see also, Patrick Fairbairn, **The Revelation of Law in Scripture,** Zondervan Publishing House, 1957.

CHRISTOLOGY
CHRIST'S PERSON AND WORK

HENGSTENBERG, ERNST WILHELM. **Christology of the Old Testament.** Grand Rapids: Kregel Publications, 1977.

A complete examination of all major Messianic passages of Scripture in the Old Testament. This classic work refutes several of the radical views of liberal scholars. Excellent. For a good smaller work, see also, James A. Borland, **Christ in the Old Testament,** Moody Press, 1978.

LAWLOR, GEORGE. **When God Became Man.** Chicago: Moody Press, 1978.

This brief work is valuable for its recent scholarship on the person and work of Christ. For another good work, see also, John F. Walvoord, **Jesus Christ Our Lord,** Moody Press, 1969.

LONGENECKER, RICHARD NORMAN. **The Christology of Early Jewish Christianity.** London: SCM Press, 1970.

A rare work portraying the Jewish Messianic expectation during the silent years of the Bible. This is a very helpful study.

VINE, WILLIAM EDWY. **The Divine Sonship of Christ.** Minneapolis: Klock and Klock Christian Publishers, 1979.

A study of the uniqueness of Christ's person and work with

an excellent vindication of Christ's deity and unique relationship with God the Father. Practical and helpful.

WARFIELD, BENJAMIN BRECKENRIDGE. **The Person and Work of Christ.** Philadelphia: Presbyterian and Reformed Publishing House Co., 1950.

Warfield's study on the Person and work of Christ is a true classic. It is probably one of the best works on Christology. For another smaller work, see also, John Owen, **The Glory of Christ,** Moody Press, 1949.

THE ATONEMENT

FORSYTH, PETER TAYLOR. **The Cruciality of the Cross.** Grand Rapids: Wm. B. Eerdmans Publishing Co., 1966.

In a day when the atonement in the New Testament is being challenged, this work defends its central place. For another good older work, see also, John S. Lidgett, **The Biblical Doctrine of the Atonement,** Klock and Klock Christian Publishers, 1979.

MARSH, FREDERICK EDWARD. **Why Did Christ Die?** Grand Rapids: Kregel Publications, 1985.

A sound exposition on the various practical and theological aspects of the atonement. Four common errors regarding the atonement are examined carefully. This work has some excellent homiletical values. For an older classic work, see also, James Denney, **The Death of Christ,** Klock and Klock Christian Publishers, 1979.

MORRIS, LEON. **The Cross in the New Testament,** Grand Rapids: Wm. B. Eerdmans Publishing Co., 1964.

This study on the death of Christ is one of the finest exegetical works in print today. Another excellent book from a New Testament scholar.

SMEATON, GEORGE. **The Apostle's Doctrine of the Atonement.** Grand Rapids: Zondervan Publishing House, 1957.

This classic work on the atonement was first published in 1870. It is a thorough study of the whole New Testament evidence bearing on this cardinal doctrine. For the author's sequel to this excellent study, see also, George Smeaton, **The Doctrine of the Atonement as Taught by Jesus Christ Himself,** Zondervan Publishing House, 1957.

BIRTH OF CHRIST

FEINBURG, CHARLES LEE. **Is the Virgin Birth in the Old Testament?** Whittier, Calif.: Emeth Publications, 1967.

One of the rare works on the Virgin Birth that is completely devoted to the Old Testament. Feinburg covers all of the important verses on this important study. Evangelical.

LIDDON, HENRY PARRY, AND JAMES ORR. **The Birth of Christ.** Minneapolis: Klock and Klock Christian Publishers, 1980.

This excellent work comprises Liddon's exposition on Luke chapter 1 and Orr's invaluable study on the virgin birth. These studies treat the biblical and theological aspects of the birth of Christ.

MACHEN, JOHN GRESHAM. **Virgin Birth of Christ.** Grand Rapids: Baker Book House, 1967.

Machen's excellent work on the virgin birth is rapidly becoming a classic. For a more modern approach, see also, Howard A. Hanke, **The Validity of the Virgin Birth.** Zondervan Publishing House, 1963.

MORRIS, LEON. **The Story of the Christ Child.** Grand Rapids: Wm. B. Eerdmans Publishing Co., 1960.

An excellent devotional study on the nativity stories as revealed in Matthew and Luke. For a more extensive study, see also, Robert G. Gromacki, **The Virgin Birth: Doctrine of Deity,** Thomas Nelson Publishers, 1974.

THE LIFE OF CHRIST

ANDREWS, SAMUEL J. **The Life of Our Lord Upon the Earth.** Grand Rapids: Zondervan Publishing House, 1954.

A historical, chronological, and geographical study of the life of Christ. This is considered one of the great classics on Christ's earthly life. Highly regarded by Dr. Wilber M. Smith.

BLAIKIE, W. G. AND ROBERT LAW. **The Inner Life of Christ.** Minneapolis: Klock and Klock Christian Publishers, 1979.

A combination of two older works—**Glimpses of the Inner Life of our Lord** and **The Emotions of Jesus.** These two excellent works had been out of print for several years, but now they are complete in one volume. For another excellent devotional work, see also, Alexander Whyte, **The Walk, Conversation and Character of Jesus Christ Our Lord,** Zondervan Publishing House, 1953.

CLOW, WILLIAM MACCALLUM. **The Day of the Cross.** Rev. ed. Grand Rapids: Baker Book House, 1954.

Clow was an excellent preacher. In this volume, he describes the Bible characters, circumstances and events at the day of the crucifixion. All of his books of sermons are helpful. For another good work, see also, William M. Clow, **The Secret of the Lord,** Baker Book House, 1955.

CULVER, ROBERT DUNCAN. **The Life of Christ.** Grand Rapids: Baker Book House, 1976.

This is one of Culver's best writings. In this work, he portrays the life of Christ in a practical and interesting manner. For a good chronological study, see, Harold W. Hoehner, **Chronological Aspects of the Life of Christ,** Zondervan Publishing House, 1977.

DALMAN, GUSTOF HERMANN. **The Words of Christ.** Minneapolis: Klock and Klock Christian Publishers, 1979.

An excellent volume on topics like; "Son of Man," "Son of God," "Christ," and "Son of David." For another classic reprint, see also, Rudolf E. Stier, **Words of the Risen Christ,** Klock and Klock Christian Publishers, 1979.

EDERSHEIM, ALFRED. **The Life and Times of Jesus the Messiah.** 2 vols. Grand Rapids: Wm. B. Eerdmans Publishing Co., 1962.

No serious minister or Bible student will want to be without this classic work. This is probably the best study on the life of Christ that has ever been published. Excellent.

FARRAR, FREDERICK WILLIAM. **The Life of Christ.** Portland, Ore.: Fountain Publications, 1964.

A work that is highly regarded by Charles H. Spurgeon. This well-illustrated edition of the life of Christ has been well accepted for years. Now available from Klock and Klock Christian Publishers.

FAWCETT, JOHN. **Christ Precious to Those That Believe.** Minneapolis: Klock and Klock Christian Publishers, 1978.

A rich devotional work on the love and faith relationship between the believer and his Lord. For another basic work, see also, Archibald T. Robertson, **Epochs in the Life of Jesus,** Charles Scribner's Sons, 1913. Now available in paperback from Broadman Press.

HARRIS, JOHN. **The Teaching Methods of Christ: Characteristics of Our Lord's Ministry.** Minneapolis: Klock and Klock Christian Publishers, 1980.

This thoroughly written work deals with studies on Christ's teaching methods and the training of His disciples. A carefully written work. For a study on the "pastoral methods" employed by Christ, see also, William G. Blaikie, **The Public Ministry of Christ,** Klock and Klock Christian Publishers, 1980.

LANGE, JOHN PETER. **The Life of the Lord Jesus Christ.** 4 vols. Grand Rapids: Zondervan Publishing House, n. d.

This classic work is based on the German edition that was published 1844–47. One of the most extensive studies on the Life of Christ. For a concise, more up-to-date work, see also, David L. McKenna, **The Jesus Model,** Word Books, 1977.

MACARTNEY, CLARENCE EDWARD NOBLE. **Twelve Great Questions about Christ.** Grand Rapids: Baker Book House, 1956.

Practical expository messages on questions as found in the gospels. For some other good homiletical works, see also, Clovis G. Chappell, **Faces About the Cross,** Abingdon Press, 1952 and **The Seven Words,** Abingdon press, 1946. Both of these books are available in paperback from Baker Book House.

MORGAN, GEORGE CAMPBELL. **The Crises of the Christ.** London: Pickering and Inglis, 1963.

A practical examination of the life of Christ as the accomplishment of a Divine work. Excellent. For another helpful study, see also, George C. Morgan, **The Teaching of Christ,** Pickering and Inglis, n. d.

STALKER, JAMES. **The Life of Christ.** Westwood, N. J.: Fleming H. Revell Co., 1949.

Even though this is a basic work on the life of Christ, it is a classic. For another excellent work, see also, James Stalker, **Christ Our Example,** Zondervan Publishing House, 1960.

NATURES OF CHRIST

ANDREWS, SAMUEL J., AND E. H. GRIFFORD. **Man and the Incarnation and The Incarnation: A Study of Philippians 2 and Psalm 110.** Minneapolis: Klock and Klock Christian Publishers, 1980.

An excellent combination of two classic works on the incarnation. This book shows that Jesus Christ is the incarnate Son of God—very God and very man.

LIDDON, HENRY PARRY. **The Divinity of Our Lord.** London: Pickering and Inglis, reprint.

A classic reprint on the Divinity of Christ. These outstanding lectures were preached before the University of Oxford in 1866. For another good work, see also, Benjamin B. Warfield, **The Lord of Glory,** Zondervan Publishing House, n. d.

MORRIS, LEON. **The Lord From Heaven.** London: Inter-Varsity Press, 1958.

This work is valuable because of its recent scholarship on the deity and humanity of Christ. Practical. For another good work, see also, Wilber M. Smith, **The Supernaturalness of Christ: Can We Still Believe in It?** W. A. Wilde Co., 1954.

SUFFERINGS OF CHRIST

BRUCE, ALEXANDER BALMAIN. **The Humiliation of Christ.** Grand Rapids: Wm. B. Eerdmans Publishing Co., 1955.

A compelling work that deepens and sharpens our perceptions of the sufferings of Christ. In addition, Bruce serves as a reliable guide in the criticism of the various theories of Christ as Lord and Redeemer. For another excellent work, see also, F. W. Krummacher, **The Suffering Saviour,** Moody Press, 1947.

SCHILDER, KLAAS. Christ in His Suffering. Translated by Henry Zylstra. Grand Rapids: Wm. B. Eerdmans Publishing Co., 1938.

This classic work deals with Christ's distress during the beginning stages and ends with Gethsemane. Highly regarded by Harold J. Ockenga. This work is now available in 1 of 3 volumes, under the title, **The Trilogy,** from Klock and Klock Christian Publishers.

TRIAL OF CHRIST

CHANDLER, WALTER M. **The Trial of Jesus: From a Lawyer's Standpoint.** Atlanta, GA: Harrison Co., 1972.

A lawyer's analysis and evaluation of Christ's Hebrew and Roman trials. This work is interesting and unique in the way it approaches this subject.

INNES, ALEXANDER T., AND FRANK J. POWELL. **The Trial of Christ.** Minneapolis: Klock and Klock Christian Publishers, 1980.

An excellent combination of two works that trace the order of events of Christ's trials and death. For another more popular work, see also, James Stalker, **The Trial and Death of Jesus Christ,** Zondervan Publishing House, 1966.

SCHILDER, KLAAS. **Christ on Trial.** Translated by Henry Zylstra. Grand Rapids: Wm. B. Eerdmans Publishing Co., 1939.

This classic work covers the events of the night of Christ's betrayal to His actual condemnation. This important work is now available, in 1 of 3 volumes, under the title, **The Trilogy,** from Klock and Klock Christian Publishers.

CRUCIFIXION OF CHRIST

KUYPER, ABRAHAM. **The Death and Resurrection of Christ.** Translated by Henry Zylstra. Grand Rapids: Zondervan Publishing House, 1960.

An important study on the death and resurrection of Christ. It was first published in 1888. This work could now be called a true classic.

SCHILDER, KLAAS. **Christ Crucified.** Translated by Henry Zylstra. Grand Rapids: Wm. B. Eerdmans Publishing Co., 1940.

Schilder's works on the life of Christ are loaded with sermon material. This study on the crucifixion of Christ is a classic. This important book is now available, in 1 of 3 volumes, under the title, **The Trilogy,** from Klock and Klock Christian Publishers.

SMITH, WILBER MOOREHEAD. **A Treasury of Great Sermons on the Death of Christ.** Grand Rapids: Baker Book House, 1970.

The expositor will find a goldmine of helpful sermon material in this fine book. Smith gleans messages on the death of Christ by great men of the past and present. For another helpful work, see also, Leon Morris, **The Story of the Cross,** Wm. B. Eerdmans Publishing Co., 1957.

RESURRECTION OF CHRIST

MOULE, HANDLEY CARR GLYN, AND JAMES ORR. **The Resurrection of Christ.** Minneapolis: Klock and Klock Christian Publishers, 1980.

A rare combination of two classic works on the bodily resurrection of Christ as described in John 20 and 21. The author's then relate the importance of this historical event to the doctrinal issues of today. For a basic work on the resurrection see also, Merrill C. Tenney, **The Vital Heart of Christianity,** Zondervan Publishing House, 1964.

SIMPSON, WILLIAM JOHN SPARROW. **The Resurrection and the Christian Faith.** Grand Rapids: Zondervan Publishing House, 1968.

This work is highly regarded by Dr. Wilber M. Smith. Of all the works on the resurrection of Christ, this study by Simpson, is one of the best. An excellent doctrinal treatment.

POST-RESURRECTION OF CHRIST

MACLAREN, ALEXANDER, AND HENRY BARCLAY SWEETE. **The Post-Resurrection Ministry of Christ.** Minneapolis: Klock and Klock Christian Publishers, 1980.

An excellent combination of the post-resurrection appearances of Christ by two outstanding authors. These two books have been uniquely blended together to form a valuable study on this subject.

ASCENSION OF CHRIST

MILLIGAN, WILLIAM. **The Ascension of Christ.** Minneapolis: Klock and Klock Christian Publishers, 1980.

A classic work on the ascension of Christ. Good books on this subject are difficult to find. For another good work, see also, Carl Brumback, **Accent on the Ascension!,** Gospel Publishing House, 1955.

ANTHROPOLOGY

EDWARDS, JONATHAN. **Original Sin.** The Works of Jonathan Edwards. New Haven: Yale University Press, 1970.

A helpful work on the Calvinistic view of sin by an outstanding theologian. This book was first published in 1758.

LAIDLAW, JOHN. **The Biblical Doctrine of Man.** Minneapolis: Klock and Klock Christian Publishers, 1980.

A true classic on Christian anthropology. This work was first published in 1937 and is still considered to be one of Laidlaw's best writings.

MACHEN, JOHN GRESHAM. **The Christian View of Man.** Banner of Truth Trust, 1965.

This work by Machen is a classic study on anthropology. Excellent. For another excellent study, see also, James Orr, **God's Image in Man and Its Defacement in the Light of Modern Denials,** Wm. B. Eerdmans Publishing Co., 1948.

MORGAN, GEORGE CAMPBELL. **The Voice of the Devil.** London: Pickering and Inglis, n. d.

In this interesting series of sermons, Morgan presents Satan's method in tempting man to sin. In addition, he shows how one can overcome these temptations from biblical examples found in the Word of God.

SAUER, ERICH ERNST. **The King of the Earth: The Nobility of Man according to the Bible and Science.** Grand Rapids: Wm. B. Eerdmans Publishing Co., 1962.

A helpful study that shows how man fell and how he can be brought back into a right relationship with God. For another good study, see also, Aiden W. Tozer, **Man: The Dwelling Place of God,** Christian Publications, 1966.

SALVATION OF MAN

BAXTER, JAMES SIDLOW. **God So Loved.** Grand Rapids: Zondervan Publishing House, 1960.

This excellent study on John 3:16 is practical and expository. For another good homiletical work on redemption, see also, Oswald Chambers, **The Psychology of Redemption,** Christian Literature Crusade, 1955.

CHAFER, LEWIS SPERRY. **He That Is Spiritual.** Grand Rapids: Zondervan Publishing House, 1965.

An outstanding exposition on the spirituality of the believer.

For another good work, see also, Lewis S. Chafer, **Grace,** Zondervan Publishing House, 1965. Practical.

DENNEY, JAMES. **The Christian Doctrine of Reconciliation.** London: James Clarke and Co., 1959.

This highly regarded work has now been reprinted by Klock and Klock Christian Publishers. Most all of Denney's works are of the utmost value.

EDWARDS, JONATHAN. **Freedom of the Will.** Edited by Paul Ramsey. New Haven: Yale University Press, 1957.

A classic work regarding the freedom of the will and human determinism. For another good older work, see also, Jonathan Edwards, **The History of Redemption,** Sovereign Grace Book Club, 1959.

FLETCHER, JOHN. **Christ Manifested.** Fort Washington, Penn.: Christian Literature Crusade, 1968.

This deeply devotional work is hailed by some as a spiritual classic. A highly regarded book recommended by D. Martyn Lloyd-Jones. For another good work, see also, Adonirum J. Gordon, **The Two-Fold Life.** Fleming H. Revell, Co., 1883.

FINNEY, CHARLES GRANDISON. **Sanctification.** Fort Washington, Penn.: Christian Literature Crusade, 1963.

An important work on the doctrine of sanctification by a challenging preacher. Arminian. For another good Arminian work, see also, William E. R. Sangster, **The Path to Perfection,** Hodder and Stoughton, 1943.

LUTHER, MARTIN. **The Bondage of the Will.** Translated by J. I. Packer and O. R. Johnston. Westwood, N. J.: Fleming H. Revell Co., 1957.

This is one of Luther's best contributions to this area of study. An important work that responds to the diatribe of Erasmus.

MACHEN, JOHN GRESHAM. **What Is Faith?** Grand Rapids: Wm. B. Eerdmans Publishing Co., 1962.

An outstanding, thorough discussion of the nature of faith in its plainest and highest manifestation as revealed in the New Testament. For another helpful work, see also, John G. Machen, **What is Christianity: And Other Addresses,** Wm. B. Eerdmans Publishing Co., 1951.

MURRAY, ANDREW. **Holy in Christ.** Grand Rapids: Zondervan Publishing House, 1962.

In this devotional work, Murray presents a true picture of the meaning of "holiness." For another excellent work on this subject, see also, J. C. Ryle, **Holiness: Its Nature, Hindrances, Difficulties, and Roots.** Kregel Publications, 1956. Good preaching material.

OWEN, JOHN. **The Doctrine of Justification by Faith.** London: Banner of Truth Trust, 1959.

This excellent work was first published in 1677. Owen was an outstanding Puritan writer. Calvinistic. For a more modern treatment, see also, Gerritt C. Berkouwer, **Faith and Justification,** Wm. B. Eerdmans Publishing Co., 1954. Calvinistic.

SAUER, ERICH ERNST. **The Dawn of World Redemption.** Translated by G. H. Lang. Grand Rapids: Wm. B. Eerdmans Publishing, Co., 1951.

An excellent study of salvation as revealed in the Old Testament. For another outstanding companion work, see also, Erich E. Sauer, **The Triumph of the Crucified,** Wm. B. Eerdmans Publishing Co., 1951. Focuses on salvation as revealed in the New Testament.

SHANK, ROBERT. **Elect in the Son: A Study of the Doctrine of Election.** Springfield, MO.: Westcott Publishers, 1971.

This is an important study from an Arminian point of view. For a balanced approach to the study of election, this work is helpful.

————. **Life in the Son: A Study of the Doctrine of Perseverance.** 2d ed. Springfield, MO.: Westcott Publishers, 1961.

The most important work to appear in several years from an Arminian point of view. A real challenge to the doctrine of eternal security. For another good Arminian writer on this subject, see also, Guy Duty, **If Ye Continue,** Bethany Fellowship, 1966.

WESTCOTT, FREDERICK BROOKE. **The Biblical Doctrine of Justification.** Minneapolis: Klock and Klock Christian Publishers, 1980.

An important work that is based upon Paul's Roman and Galatian letters. This volume is thorough in exegesis. For another good evangelical work, see also, James Buchanan, **The Doctrine of Justification,** Baker Book House, 1955.

SPIRIT BEINGS

ANDREWS, SAMUEL. **Christianity and Anti-Christianity in Their Final Conflict.** Minneapolis: Klock and Klock Christian Publishers, 1980.

A great work on the study of the Antichrist and the apostacy of the last days. Highly recommended by Dr. Wilber M. Smith. For another good work, see also, Arthur W. Pink, **The Antichrist,** Klock and Klock Christian Publishers, 1979.

BARNHOUSE, DONALD GREY. **The Invisible War.** Grand Rapids: Zondervan Publishing House, 1965.

This informative study reveals the conflict between good and evil in the spiritual world. For a more comprehensive work, see also, C. Fred Dickason, **Angels, Elect and Evil.** Moody Press, 1975.

BOUNDS, EDWARD MCKENDREE. **Satan: His Personality, Power and Overthrow.** Grand Rapids: Baker Book House, 1963.

An excellent work on the study of Satan. Bounds has several devotional books that are valuable. For a more recent work, see also, Hal Lindsey and Carole C. Carlson, **Satan is Alive and Well on Planet Earth,** Zondervan Publishing House, 1972.

GAEBELEIN, ARNO C. **The Angels of God.** Grand Rapids: Zondervan Publishing House, 1969.

This is one of the better works on the study of angels. For a more recent study, see also, William F. Graham, **Angels: God's Secret Agents,** Doubleday and Co., 1975.

PENTECOST, JOHN DWIGHT. **Your Adversary the Devil.** Grand Rapids: Zondervan Publishing House, 1969.

A series of messages following Satan's origin, life and ministry, and future punishment. Practical. For another good study, see also, Lewis S. Chafer, **Satan: His Motives and Methods.** Zondervan Publishing House, 1964.

WIERSBE, WARREN W. **The Strategy of Satan: How to**

Detect and Defeat Him. Wheaton, IL: Tyndale House Publishers, 1979.

In this recent study, Wiersbe deals with Satan's tactics in a practical manner. This book will be a helpful guide for preaching a series of messages on Satan. For a good older study, see also, John L. Nevius, **Demon Possession,** Kregel Publications, 1986.

ESCHATOLOGY

ANDERSON, SIR ROBERT. **The Coming Prince.** Grand Rapids: Kregel Publications, 1963.

One of the most detailed works ever written on Daniel's Seventieth Week and the coming Antichrist. This volume can now be purchased in paperback.

BARON, DAVID. **Israel in the Plan of God.** Grand Rapids: Kregel Publications, 1982.

This book deals with the four major passages of Scripture that deal exclusively with Israel's history. For a more recent study, see also, John F. Walvoord, **Israel in Prophecy,** Zondervan Publishing House, 1962.

BOICE, JAMES MONTGOMERY. **God and History.** Vol. IV, Foundations of the Christian Faith. Downers Grove, IL.: Inter-Varsity Press, 1981.

An excellent modern study of eschatology by an evangelical, Presbyterian minister. For a more extensive work, see also, Alexander Keith, **Christian Evidences: Fulfilled Bible Prophecy,** Klock and Klock Christian Publishers, 1980.

IRONSIDE, HENRY ALLAN, AND FORD C. OTTMAN. **Studies in Biblical Eschatology.** Minneapolis: Klock and Klock Christian Publishers, 1981.

These two important eschatological studies of Ironside and Ottman have now been brought together in one volume. For another good study, see also, Frederick A. Tatford, **God's Program of the Ages,** Kregel Publications, 1967. Premillennial.

PETERS, GEORGE NATHANIEL HENRY. **The Theocratic Kingdom of Our Lord Jesus the Christ, as Covenanted in**

the Old Testament and Presented in the New Testament.
Grand Rapids: Kregel Publications, 1979.

A truly monumental work on the study of Bible prophecy.
This work is a classic that was first published in 1884. Highly
recommended by Dr. Wilber M. Smith. Premillennial. For another comprehensive study, see also, John D. Pentecost,
Things to Come, Zondervan Publishing House, 1958. Premillennial.

SHANK, ROBERT. **Until: The Coming of Messiah and His
Kingdom.** Springfield, MO.: Westcott Publishers, 1982.

A good Premillennial study on the Messianic prophecies.
This work is complete and up-to-date. For a good older study,
see also, P. J. Gloag and F. J. Delitzsch, **The Messiahship of
Christ,** Klock and Klock Christian Publishers, 1980.

THE RAPTURE/SECOND COMING

BLACKSTONE, WILLIAM E. **Jesus Is Coming.**
Westwood, N. J.: Fleming H. Revell Co., 1908.

A classic work on the return of Jesus Christ. Blackstone
packs a lot of helpful information into this little volume. Premillennial. For another standard work, see also, Rene Pache,
The Return of Jesus Christ, Translated by William S. LaSor,
Moody Press, 1955.

WALVOORD, JOHN FLIPSE. **The Rapture Question.** Revised and enlarged ed. Grand Rapids: Zondervan Publishing
House, 1979.

Walvoord believes in a pretribulation rapture. This work is
very helpful from this point of view. For a work with the
posttribulation view, see also, Robert H. Gundry, **The Church
and the Tribulation,** Zondervan Publishing House, 1973.

———. **The Blessed Hope and the Tribulation: A Biblical
and Historical Study of Posttribulationism.** Grand Rapids: Zondervan Publishing House, 1976.

A valuable study on the four main teachings within posttribulationism. Walvoord concludes that the pretribulation view
of the rapture is the most Scriptural interpretation.

THE MILLENNIUM

MCCLAIN, ALVA J. **The Greatness of the Kingdom.** Grand Rapids: Zondervan Publishing House, 1959.

McClain's work on eschatology is outstanding. For another good modern study, see also, John F. Walvoord, **The Millennial Kingdom,** Rev. ed., Dunham Publishing Co., 1965. Premillennial.

WEST, NATHANIEL. **The Thousand Years in Both Testaments.** Grand Rapids: Kregel Publications, n. d.

A classic treatment on the study of the millennium as revealed in the Old and New Testaments. Highly recommended by Dr. Wilber M. Smith.

FUTURE STATE

PACHE, RENE. **The Future Life.** Translated by Helen I. Needham. Chicago: Moody Press, 1962.

This modern study of the future life covers the biblical teaching on man and his destiny, death, the world of spirits, the resurrection, hell and heaven. A very helpful work.

IMMORTALITY

BOETTNER, LORAINE. **Immortality.** 7th ed. Philadelphia: Presbyterian and Reformed Publishing Co., 1958.

A detailed work dealing with the entire area of immortality. This is one of the best works on this subject. Evangelical. For a good homiletical work, see also, Clarence E. Macartney, **Putting on Immortality,** Fleming H. Revell Co., 1926.

SALMOND, S. D. F. **The Biblical Doctrine of Immortality.** Minneapolis: Klock and Klock Christian Publishers, 1980.

This classic work comprises the William Cunningham Lectures of several years ago. Dr. Salmond was fully abreast of Christian as well as pagan literature. An excellent study of the biblical teaching of immortality.

HEAVEN/HELL

BAXTER, RICHARD. **The Saint's Everlasting Rest.** Grand Rapids: Zondervan Publishing House, 1962.

A valuable classic on the study of heaven. For another good work, see also, Edward M. Bounds, **Heaven: A Place, A City, A Home,** Baker Book House, 1966.

SHEDD, WILLIAM GREENOUGH THAYER. **The Doctrine of Endless Punishment.** Minneapolis: Klock and Klock Christian Publishers, 1980.

A classic reprint on the study of the teaching on the future of unbelievers. While many today are denying the teaching of endless punishment, Shedd holds to this doctrine from an evangelical perspective.

SMITH, WILBER MOOREHEAD. **The Biblical Doctrine of Heaven.** Chicago: Moody Press, 1968.

This is an excellent detailed study on the biblical doctrine of heaven. A valuable evangelical contribution to the field of Eschatology.

JUDGEMENT

MORRIS, LEON. **The Biblical Doctrine of Judgement.** London: Tyndale Press, 1960.

This evangelical writer presents an Old and New Testament study of judgement. He gets at the heart of the meaning of words that are used to express the judgement. Excellent.

APOLOGETICS

BRUCE, FREDERICK FYVIE. **The Defense of the Gospel in the New Testament.** Revised ed. Grand Rapids: Wm. B. Eerdmans Publishing Co., 1977.

These excellent lectures defend the integrity of the New Testament message. Evangelical. For another good older work, see also, Alexander Balmain Bruce, **Apologetics: or Christianity Defensively Stated,** T. and T. Clark, 1927.

LEWIS, CLIVE STAPLES. **Mere Christianity.** London: Macmillan Co., 1952.

A vigorous defense of Christianity by an outstanding Christian writer. For a more recent evangelical work, see also, Paul E. Little, **Know Why You Believe,** Scripture Press Publications, 1967.

MACHEN, JOHN GRESHAM. **Christian Faith in the Modern World.** Grand Rapids: Wm. B. Eerdmans Publishing Co., 1967.

A brilliant defense of Scriptural authority on the various subjects of apologetics. For another good older work, see also, William H. G. Thomas, **Christianity is Christ,** Longmans Green and Co., 1925.

MCDOWELL, JOSH, (comp.) **Evidence That Demands a Verdict: Historical Evidences for the Christian Faith.** Revised ed. San Bernardino, CA: Here's Life Publishers, 1979.

An excellent evangelical study on apologetics. This work shows painstaking research. For another good volume, see also, Josh McDowell, **More Evidence That Demands a Verdict,** Revised ed., Here's Life Publishers, 1981.

SMITH, WILBER MOOREHEAD. **Therefore Stand.** Boston: W. A. Wilde Co., 1945.

This work has never been superseded. It stands among the best in the field of apologetics. Evangelical. Now available from Baker Book House.

THOMAS, J. D. **Facts and Faith.** Vol. 1. Abilene, Texas: Biblical Research Press, 1965.

An excellent treatment of reason, science and faith. This author believes that the Bible deserves a more serious consideration as God's exact revelation than it is now receiving. For another good work, see also, Henry M. Morris, **Many Infallible Proofs,** Creation-Life Publishers, 1974.

Section Four

Books on Pastoral Theology

Books on pastoral theology are extremely helpful in the daily tasks of the ministry. Unfortunately, the average minister has a tendency to stop reading this type of book upon completion of his formal training. It is important that every minister have an overall picture of the field of practical theology if he is to be effective in his high calling as the man of God.

In this section, it was decided to emphasize books that are practical rather than the theoretical aspects of the work of the preacher. With all the new books being published on pastoral theology, selective reading on the part of the busy minister becomes increasingly important. Hence, there is a need for a book like this to help each person survey the most important publications in this field of study. It is obvious that a minister does not have time to fumble through a great number of second rate books to find the facts and information that he needs in the preparation of sermons, lessons, and counseling.

Many pastors of my acquaintance overlook the value of good sermon collections. Samuel Johnson once said that "a library must be imperfect if it has not a numerous collection of sermons." This section will help remedy this deficiency in many pastor's libraries. It is vitally important that a minister be exposed to the most important preachers in church history.

Finally, recognizing the need for good counsel, several books have been selected in the area of pastoral care and counseling. Since the average minister is plunged into all kinds of distressing situations, he will want to be well-equipped to deal with a variety of human needs.

PASTORAL THEOLOGY

Baker's Dictionary of Practical Theology. Edited by Ralph G. Turnbull. Grand Rapids: Baker Book House, 1967.
This work has some outstanding articles on pastoral theology. It is broad in scope and basically evangelical in theology. An excellent reference handbook.
BLACKWOOD, ANDREW WATTERSON. **Pastoral Work.** Grand Rapids: Baker Book House, 1954.

A practical book on pastoring. Blackwood has written many helpful works in the field of pastoral theology. Now available in paperback from Baker Book House. For another good work, see also, Andrew W. Blackwood, **Pastoral Leadership,** Abingdon-Cokesbury Press, 1949. Now available in paperback from Baker Book House.

KENT, HOMER AUSTIN, SR. **The Pastor and His Work.** Chicago: Moody Press, 1963.

This is a standard text on pastoral theology. Kent has shared much of his practical experience as a pastor. For another good, but somewhat dated book, see also, John C. Thiessen, **Pastoring the Smaller Church,** Zondervan Publishing House, 1962.

MORGAN, GEORGE CAMPBELL. **The Ministry of the Word.** Grand Rapids: Baker Book House, 1970.

Morgan was an outstanding expositor of God's Word. This work on the task of pastoring is excellent. See also, Archibald T. Robertson, **The Glory of the Ministry: Paul's Exaltation in Preaching,** Baker Book House, 1967. See comments under II Corinthians.

SPURGEON, CHARLES HADDON. **Lectures to My Students.** Grand Rapids: Zondervan Publishing House, 1955.

A classic series of lectures on every facet of the pastor's life. This work was first published, 1874–94 and yet it is still extremely valuable to the minister today. Highly recommended by Dr. Wilber M. Smith.

STOTT, JOHN ROBERT WALMSEY. **The Preacher's Portrait.** Grand Rapids: Wm. B. Eerdmans Publishing Co., 1964.

In this volume, Stott points out the biblical qualifications of the minister. This is an excellent study on the man and his mission as a preacher. For another good work, see also, Ralph G. Turnball, **The Preacher's Heritage, Task and Resources,** Baker Book House, 1968.

ZIMMERMAN, THOMAS F. et al. **And He Gave Pastors.** Springfield, MO.: Gospel Publishing House, 1978.

A comprehensive manual that discusses the pastor and his relationship to his Lord, his family, church, his affiliation, his counseling, finances, and more. This is a very practical work.

PREACHING AND HOMILETICS

BLACKWOOD, ANDREW WATTERSON. **The Preparation of Sermons.** New York: Abingdon Press, 1948.
Blackwood's books on preaching and homiletics are extremely valuable. This is a helpful volume in sermon preparation. For another good work, see also, Andrew W. Blackwood, **Planning a Year's Pulpit Work,** Abingdon Press, 1942.

BRAGA, JAMES. **How to Prepare Bible Messages.** Rev. ed. Portland, OR.: Multnomah Press, 1982.
An extremely helpful and practical manual on homiletics. This is one of the best books on sermon preparation. For another good older work, see also, William Evans, **How to Prepare Sermons and Gospel Addresses,** Moody Press, 1913.

BROADUS, JOHN ALBERT. **On the Preparation and Delivery of Sermons.** Rev. ed. by Jesse Burton Weatherspoon. New York: Harper and Row, 1943.
This work was first published in 1870. It is considered a classic on the fundamentals of homiletics. Some areas are technical, but this work is still valuable. For a more up-to-date study, see also, Johann M. Reu, **Homiletics: A Manual of the Theory and Practice of Preaching,** Baker Book House, 1967.

BROOKS, PHILLIPS. **Lectures on Preaching.** Grand Rapids: Zondervan Publishing House, n. d.
Brooks delivered these eight lectures on preaching at Yale University in 1877. All preachers need to study the famous Lyman Beecher lectures on preaching. This work by Brooks is excellent. For another good book on the Lyman Beecher lectures on preaching, see also, John Hall, **God's Word Through Preaching,** Baker Book House, 1979.

DEMARAY, DONALD E. **An Introduction to Homiletics.** Grand Rapids: Baker Book House, 1974.
A very helpful study in the field of homiletics. Demaray discusses with authority, insight, and clarity the many aspects of sermon-making and delivery. For another helpful work, see also, William E. R. Sangster, **The Craft of Sermon Construction,** Westminster Press, 1951.

JONES, EDGAR DE WITT. **The Royalty of the Pulpit.** New York: Harper and Brothers, 1951.

This outstanding book focuses on the men who delivered the famous Lyman Beecher lectures on preaching. If you are serious about studying the Yale lectures, this work is a must. For another good book on the Lyman Beecher lectures on Preaching, see also, Paul Scherer, **For We Have This Treasure,** Harper and Row, 1965. Unfortunately, many of these Lyman Beecher lectures are now out of print. Try to buy them whenever and wherever you can.

LLOYD-JONES, DAVID MARTYN. **Preaching and Preachers.** Grand Rapids: Zondervan Publishing House, 1972.

Dr. D. Martyn Lloyd-Jones has been described as "the last of the preachers." He demonstrates that the work of preaching is the highest and the greatest calling to which anyone can ever be called. Excellent and challenging.

PERRY, LLOYD MERLE. **Biblical Preaching for Today's World.** Chicago: Moody Press, 1973.

A fresh treatment on the importance and variety of biblical preaching from one of the best homiletical teachers in America today. For another good work, see also, Lloyd M. Perry, **Manual for Biblical Preaching,** Baker Book House, 1965.

STALKER, JAMES. **The Preacher and His Models.**Grand Rapids: Baker Book House, 1967.

These messages were given as the Yale Lectures in 1891. Stalker uses the prophet Isaiah and the apostle Paul as models for preaching. For another good work, see also, James S. Stewart, **Heralds of God.** Charles Scribner's Sons, 1946.

HISTORY OF PREACHING

DARGAN, EDWIN CHARLES. **A History of Preaching.** 2 vols. Grand Rapids: Baker Book House, 1968.

This excellent set covers the history of preaching from the Apostolic fathers to 1900. Highly recommended by Dr. Wilber M. Smith. A standard in its field. For a companion volume, see also, Ralph G. Turnball, **A History of Preaching,** Vol. 3, Baker Book House, 1974.

BIOGRAPHICAL PREACHING

BLACKWOOD, ANDREW WATTERSON. **Biographical Preaching for Today.** New York: Abingdon Press, 1953.

An excellent book telling how famous preachers of the past have used the biographical method of preaching effectively. In addition, Blackwood tells the minister how to prepare a biographical sermon and use his own imagination in applying it to people's needs. For another good work, see also, Faris D. Whitesell, **Preaching on Bible Characters,** Baker Book House, 1955.

DOCTRINAL PREACHING

BLACKWOOD, ANDREW WATTERSON. **Doctrinal Preaching for Today.** New York: Abingdon Press, 1953.

In the first part of his book, Blackwood tells why doctrine should be preached, and in the second part of the book, he tells the how of doctrinal preaching. Excellent. For another good work, see also, William E. R. Sangster, **Doctrinal Preaching: Its Neglect and Recovery,** Berean Press, 1953.

EVANGELISTIC PREACHING

PERRY, LLOYD MERLE, AND JOHN R. STRUBBER. **Evangelistic Preaching.** Chicago: Moody Press, 1979.

This practical work surveys the trends in evangelism from the earliest times to the present. A valuable book for those wanting to do true evangelistic preaching. Evangelical.

STANFIELD, V. L. **Effective Evangelistic Preaching.** Grand Rapids: Baker Book House, 1965.

Stanfield is highly qualified to give guidance in the area of evangelistic preaching. A helpful study. For another good work, see also, Faris D. Whitesell, **Evangelistic Preaching and the Old Testament,** Moody Press, 1947.

EXPOSITORY PREACHING

BLACKWOOD, ANDREW WATTERSON. **Expository Preaching for Today.** New York: Abingdon Press, 1953.
A clear explanation of the principles used to originate, develop, and maintain a forceful style of expository preaching. For another good older work, see also, F. B. Meyer, **Expository Preaching-Plans and Methods.** Zondervan Publishing House, 1954.

KOLLER, CHARLES W. **Expository Preaching without Notes.** Grand Rapids: Baker Book House, 1962.
This book stresses the why and how of expository preaching. If any minister wishes to increase his pulpit power, this work will be helpful. For another good work, see also, Faris D. Whitesell, **Power in Expository Preaching,** Fleming H. Revell Co., 1963.

UNGER, MERRILL F. **Principles of Expository Preaching.** Grand Rapids: Zondervan Publishing House, 1955.
One of the most exhaustive treatments on the subject of expository preaching. This work also has an abundance of footnotes and a helpful bibliography at the end of each chapter. For another excellent work, see also, Haddon W, Robinson, **Biblical Preaching: The Development and Delivery of Expository Messages,** Baker Book House, 1980.

WAGNER, DON M. **The Expository Method of G. Campbell Morgan.** Westwood: N. J.: Fleming H. Revell Co., 1957.
This book contains an inspiring account of the expository method of G. Campbell Morgan. For another helpful work, see also, G. Campbell Morgan, **Preaching,** Fleming H. Revell Co., 1937.

PROPHETIC PREACHING

LEAVELL, ROLAND Q. **Prophetic Preaching Then and Now.** Grand Rapids: Baker Book House, 1963.

An excellent work on the study of Old Testament preaching. The author shows that all the distressing trends of today were also prevalent in Old Testament times and denounced by the prophets.

THE MINISTER'S LIBRARY

BARBER, CYRIL J. **The Minister's Library.** 2 vols. Chicago: Moody Press, 1985.

An extensive treatment on the minister's library. Unfortunately, many of the books listed are overly technical for the average minister. In addition, much of the space is wasted with liberal works that the evangelical preacher will not use and many of the books listed are out of print. Barber shows his theological bias by ignoring many writers that have contributed greatly to the field of Christian writing. This set will be helpful to the scholar rather than to the average minister.

BROOKMAN, DAVID WAYNE. **Basic Books for the Minister's Library.** Shippensburg, Penn.: Destiny Image Publishers, 1986.

This book was written for pastors, theologians, Bible college students, seminarians and Christian workers on all levels of service. It presents a balance of different theological "slants." Most of the books that are recommended are written from an evangelical point of view. The book contains well over 1000 selected works that are considered "basic" for a minister's library. However, this is not to suggest that it is necessary to purchase every volume recommended. In this work, the author has tried to mention only books that are in print as of its writing.

(Note: For other works on the minister's library, see comments under the **bibliography** section of this book.)

THE MINISTER'S FILING SYSTEM

BROOKMAN, DAVID WAYNE. **The Minister's Practical Filing System.** Harrisonburg, VA.: Published by the author, 1983.

A simple and practical filing system that brings together in one central index, material from books, tapes, articles, notes, and transparencies. For example, once a minister has recorded his material on an index sheet on a given passage of Scripture, he can pull his index to see what is available from every source in a matter of minutes. In addition, this system shows a minister how to set up his files on every area from Church Administration to Theology. There is even a section that lists every book of the Bible for the filing of material. This file can be used topically or for expository purposes. Included in this system is a chronological index form whereby a minister can keep a log of all of his weekly activities, such as, sermons, weddings, funerals, baby dedications, baptisms and any other practical information. This if the most comprehensive filing system on the religious market today.

ILLUSTRATING SERMONS

MACPHERSON, IAN, **The Art of Illustrating Sermons.** New York: Abingdon Press, 1964.

This is one of the best books available on illustrating sermons. An excellent study. For another helpful work, see also, Louis P. Lehman, **How to Find and Develop Effective Illustrations,** Kregel Publications, 1975.

SERMON ILLUSTRATIONS

DOAN, ELEANOR. **The Speaker's Source Book.** Grand Rapids: Zondervan Publishing House, 1960.

A very helpful collection of illustrations and other sayings arranged by subject. For a good companion volume, see also,

Eleanor Doan, **The New Speaker's Source Book,** Zondervan Publishing House, 1968.

LOCKYER, HERBERT. **Last Words of Saints and Sinners.** Grand Rapids: Kregel Publicaitons, 1969.

Lockyer is an extremely practical writer on many subjects. This work provides helpful resource material in sermon preparation. For another helpful work, see also, Herbert V. Prochnow, **A Treasury of Stories, Illustrations, Epigrams, and Quotations for Ministers and Teachers,** Baker Book House, 1957. Another good source for illustrations can be found in the many books of sermons by different authors.

MACARTNEY, CLARENCE EDWARD. **Macartney's Illustrations.** New York: Abingdon-Cokesbury Press, 1945.

Macartney was a master at illustrating sermons. This work contains illustrations from the many sermons that he preached over the years. They are arranged alphabetically by sub-divisions and cross references.

CHRISTIAN POETRY

MARCHANT, JAMES (comp.). **Anthology of Jesus.** Grand Rapids: Kregel Publications, 1980.

A listing of 400 prose writings and poems relating to Christ. This list is compiled from the writings of over 200 authors. Practical.

TOZER, AIDEN WILSON. **The Christian Book of Mystical Verse.** Harrisburg, Penn.: Christian Publications, 1963.

This excellent work contains several helpful poems that deal with everyday Christian living. For another good work, see also, Oswald J. Smith, **Poems of a Lifetime,** Marshall, Morgan and Scott, 1962.

CHRISTIAN HUMOR

ARNOLD, OREN. **Snappy Steeple Stories.** Grand Rapids: Kregel Publications, 1979.

A compilation of humerous stories that preachers tell. For another helpful volume, see also, Oren Arnold, **Sourcebook of Family Humor,** Kregel Publications, 1979.

CARTWRIGHT, CHARLES. **Cartwright's Choice Chuckles.** Grand Rapids: Kregel Publications, 1968.

This book of church humor is designed to make people laugh at themselves. For another good author on Christian humor, see also, Herbert V. Procknow, **The Successful Toastmaster,** Harper and Row, 1966. This author has other helpful books on humor.

PHILLIPS, BOB. **The World's Greatest Collection of Clean Jokes.** Wheaton, IL.: Key Publishers, 1973.

This title says it all. A helpful compilation of good clean jokes. For another good book, see also, Bob Phillips, **The Last of the Good Clean Jokes,** Harvest House Publishers, 1974.

QUOTATIONS

MEAD, FRANK S. (comp.). **The Encyclopedia of Religious Quotations.** Old Tappan: N. J.:Fleming H. Revell Co., 1965.

A collection of nearly 12,000 quotes from more than 2,500 different sources on almost two hundred subjects. This excellent work is indexed by topic and author. For another helpful work, see also, F. B. Proctor, **Treasury of Quotations on Religious Subjects,** Kregel Publications, 1976.

NEAL, WILLIAM (comp.). **Concise Dictionary of Religious Quotations.** Grand Rapids: Wm. B. Eerdmans Publishing Co., 1974.

This practical work is arranged alphabetically by topic. It will be of great value to ministers. For another good work, see also, Sherwood E. Wirt and Kersten Beckstrom (comp.), **Living Quotations for Christians,** Harper and Row, 1974.

BOOKS ON BIBLE CHARACTERS

CHAPPELL, CLOVIS GILLHAM. **Sermons on Biblical Characters.** Grand Rapids: Baker Book House, 1970.

An outstanding book for the minister who wishes to preach a series of sermons on Bible characters. For another good work, see also, Clovis G. Chappell, **Familiar Failures,** Baker Book House, 1970.

————. **Surprises in the Bible.** Nashville: Abingdon Press, 1967.

This book is loaded with practical sermons about amazing people and unexpected events. For another good work, see also, Clovis G. Chappell, **Faces About the Cross,** Baker Book House, 1970.

HIEBERT, DAVID EDMOND. **Personalities Around Paul.** Chicago: Moody Press, 1973.

An excellent presentation of the men and women who ministered with the apostle Paul. For another good work, see also, Archibald T. Robertson, **Some Minor Characters in the New Testament,** Baker Book House, 1976.

LASOR, WILLIAM LANFORD. **Great Personalities of the Bible.** Westwood, N.J.: Fleming H. Revell Co., 1965.

LaSor's work provides excellent background material and good practical applications on Thirty-Six Bible characters. This book is actually two volumes in one.

MACARTNEY, CLARENCE EDWARD NOBLE. **Bible Epitaphs.** Grand Rapids: Baker Book House, 1974.

Macartney was an excellent preacher of Bible personalities. This book is a mixture of good and bad people of the Bible. A unique study. For another good work, see also, Clarence E. Macartney, **Great Interviews of Jesus,** Baker Book House, 1974.

————. **Chariots of Fire.** Grand Rapids: Baker Book House, 1977.

A practical series of sermons on eighteen minor characters of the Old and New Testament Chronicles. For another helpful volume, see also, Clarence E. Macartney, **The Greatest Questions of the Bible and Life,** Baker Book House, 1977.

————. **Sermons on Old Testament Heroes.** Grand Rapids: Baker Book House, 1977.

An excellent reprint of Bible characters on the Old Testament. This book really makes these interesting characters come alive.

WHYTE, ALEXANDER. **Bible Characters.** Grand Rapids: Zondervan Publishing House, 1967.

This is one of the best books on Bible characters to be found anywhere. Dr. Wilber M. Smith highly recommends this book to all ministers.

MEN OF THE BIBLE

CHAPPELL, CLOVIS GILLHAM. **Meet These Men.** Grand Rapids: Baker Book House, 1974.

Each of these practical messages are based on a different personality of the Bible. The author lays bare the spiritual lives of these characters. For another good companion volume, see also, Clovis G. Chappell, **Men That Count,** Baker Book House, 1967.

MACARTNEY, CLARENCE EDWARD NOBLE. **Trials of Great Men of the Bible.** New York: Abingdon Press, 1946.

This unique study explores how different men were tested in the Bible, and how they reacted to these trials. Excellent. Now available in paperback from Baker Book House.

WOMEN OF THE BIBLE

CHAPPELL, CLOVIS GILLHAM. **Feminine Faces.** New York: Abingdon Press, 1942.

An excellent work dealing with various women in the Bible. These are extremely practical messages. This book is now available in paperback from Baker Book House. For another good book on Bible women, see also, Harold J. Ockenga, **Women Who Made Bible History,** Zondervan Publishing House, 1962.

MACARTNEY, CLARENCE EDWARD NOBLE. **Great Women of the Bible.** Grand Rapids: Baker Book House, 1977.

Messages and character sketches dealing with Bible women.

A very helpful study. For another valuable reprint, see also, Clarence E. Macartney, **The Woman of Tekoah and Other Sermons on Bible Characters,** Baker Book House, 1977. (Note: Many other books on Bible characters can be found under the book of the Bible where they are located.)

BOOKS ON BIBLICAL SERMONS

FANT, CLYDE E. JR. AND WILLIAM M. PINSON, JR. **Twenty Centuries of Great Preaching: An Encyclopedia of Preaching.** 13 vols. Waco: Word Books, 1971.

This helpful set contains the sermons of men of all denominations and periods of history. Some of the sermons are of little value because of their liberal tendencies.

KERR, WILLIAM F. **Minister's Research Service.** Wheaton, IL: Tyndale House Publishers, 1972.

An excellent compilation of fifty-two expository sermons highlighting important topics that every minister will want to preach on throughout the calendar year.

MORGAN, GEORGE CAMPBELL. **The Westminster Pulpit.** 5 vols. Westwood, N.J.: Fleming H. Revell Co., n.d.

These are some of the finest examples of expository preaching to be found anywhere. This important work was highly recommended by Dr. Wilber M. Smith. For another good set, see also, Joseph Parker, **Preaching Through the Bible,** 28 vols., Baker Book House, reprint, 1956–61.

SPURGEON, CHARLES HADDON. **Treasury of the Bible.** 4 vols. Grand Rapids: Zondervan Publishing House, 1968.

This classic set contains over 2600 sermons. The print is small but the material is excellent. If you are willing to pay the price, see also, Charles H. Spurgeon, **Metropolitan Tabernacle Pulpit,** Banner of Truth Trust, 1965–.

WIERSBE, WARREN W. (comp.) **Treasury of the World's Great Sermons.** Grand Rapids: Kregel Publications, 1977.

A helpful collection of 122 outstanding sermons from 122 of the greatest preachers with a short biographical description of each preacher. Excellent. (Note: In order to save space, the author will not list a lot of books of sermons. Instead, I will list many of the best authors of sermons in alphabetical order. Most of the books by these writers are worth purchasing for your personal library. I will attempt to list only authors whose books are in print.)

BOOKS OF SERMONS BY AUTHOR

BANKS, LOUIS A.
BOREHAM, FRANK W.
BUNYAN, JOHN
CALVIN, JOHN
CLOW, WILLIAM M.
DENNEY, JAMES
EADIE, JOHN
FINNEY, CHARLES G.
GRAHAM, WILLIAM
HODGE, CHARLES
LEE, ROBERT G.
LUTHER, MARTIN
MACLAREN, ALEXANDER
MOODY, DWIGHT L.
MURRAY, ANDREW
OGILVIE, LLOYD J.
ROBERTSON, A.T.
SAPHIR, ADOLPH
SPURGEON, CHARLES H.
STOTT, J. R. W.
TAYLOR, WILLIAM M.
TRUETT, GEORGE
WHITEFIELD, GEORGE
ZODHIATES, SPIROS

BAXTER, RICHARD
BROADUS, JOHN A.
BURRELL, DAVID J.
CHALMERS, THOMAS
CRISWELL, WALLIE A.
DIXON, A. C.
EDWARDS, JONATHAN
GORDON, A. J.
GUTHRIE, THOMAS
JONES, J.D.
LIDDON, HENRY P.
MACARTNEY, C. M.
MCCHEYNE, ROBERT
MORGAN G. CAMPBELL
NEE, WATCHMAN
PARKER, JOSEPH
ROBERTSON, F. W.
SEISS, JOSEPH A.
STALKER, JAMES
SWINDOLL, CHUCK
TORREY, R. A.
WARD, C. M.
WHYTE, ALEXANDER

BEECHER, HENRY WARD
BROOKS, PHILLIPS
BUSHNELL, HORACE
CHAPPELL, CLOVIS G.
DALE, ROBERT W.
DRUMMOND, HENRY
FINDLEY, G. G.
GORDON, S. D.
HALL, JOHN
JOWETT, JOHN H.
LLOYD-JONES D. MARTYN
MACKINTOSH, C. H.
MEYER, F. B.
MORRISON, GEORGE
OCKENGA, HAROLD J.
PIERSON, A. T.
RYLE, J. C.
SIMPSON, A. B.
STEWART, JAMES S.
TALMAGE, THOMAS D.
TOZER, A. W.
WESLEY, JOHN
WIERSBE, WARREN W.

BIOGRAPHIES OF PREACHERS

ANDERSON, COURTNEY. **To The Golden Shore: The Life of Adoniram Judson.** Boston: Little, Brown and Co., 1956.

A thrilling account of the first American to start a mission in the East. For another good missionary account, see also, Frank D. Walker, **William Carey: Missionary Pioneer and Statesman,** Moody Press, 1951.

CAIRNS, EARLE E. **V. Raymond Edman: In the Presence of the King.** Chicago: Moody Press, 1972.

This is the story of an outstanding man who was a pastor, missionary, professor and college president. For another good modern biography, see also, David Poling, **Why Billy Graham?**, Zondervan Publishing House, 1977.

DALLIMORE, ARNOLD A. **George Whitefield: The Life and Times of the Great Evangelist of the Eighteenth-Century Revival.** Vol. 2. Westchester, IL: Cornerstone Books, 1979.

This is a companion volume to the author's other work on George Whitefield. A most inspiring book. Be sure to purchase volume 1 from Banner of Truth Trust.

ELLIOTT ELIZABETH. **Through the Gates of Splendor.** New York: Harper and Row, 1957.

One of the most well-known missionary stories ever recorded. Inspiring. For another good work, see also, Elizabeth Elliott, **Shadow of the Almighty,** Harper and Row, 1958.

ENGLISH, EUGENE SCHUYLER. **Ordained of the Lord: H. A. Ironside, a Biography.** Neptune, NJ: Loizeaux Brothers, 1976.

An interesting biography of a great preacher. This is a revision of the author's work of 1946. For another excellent work, see also, David J. Fant, **A. W. Tozer A Twentieth Century Prophet,** Christian Publications, 1964.

MANN, A. CHESTER. **F. B. Meyer—Preacher, Teacher, Man of God.** New York: Fleming H. Revell Co., 1929.

This interesting biography shows the far-reaching impact that Meyer had on the word through his preaching and writings. For another excellent work, see also, V. Raymond Edman, **Finney Lives On, The Man, His Revival Methods and His Message,** Fleming H. Revell Co., 1951.

LOCKYER, HERBERT. **The Man Who Changed the World.** 2 vols. Grand Rapids: Zondervan Publishing House, 1966.

An excellent study of various men who changed their world. Volume one covers men from the first through the sixteenth centuries. Volume two covers men from the seventeenth through the twentieth centuries. For another helpful work, see also, Warren Wiersbe, **Walking With the Giants: A Minister's Guide to Good Reading and Great Preaching,** Baker Book

House, 1976. (Note: Since many ministers will want to make their own choice as to what lives they would like to read, this section has been limited in the number of biographical recommendations.)

BOOKS ABOUT THE MINISTRY

BAXTER, RICHARD. **The Reformed Pastor.** Revised and edited by Hugh Martin. Richmond: John Knox Press, 1956.

This important work first appeared in 1656. It is a classic work on the pastoral ministry. For another good older work, see also, John H. Jowett, **The Preacher: His Life and Work,** Baker Book House, 1968.

BLACKWOOD, ANDREW WATTERSON. **The Growing Minister.** Nashville: Abingdon Press, 1960.

Blackwood knows the opportunities and obstacles to personal growth in the ministry. In this helpful book, he gives some practical guidelines in working toward maturity. For another helpful work, see also, Wayne E. Oates, **The Christian Pastor,** Rev. ed., Westminster Press, 1963.

BLACKWOOD, CAROLYN PHILIPS. **The Pastor's Wife.** Philadephia: Westminster Press, 1951.

An excellent book for a pastor's wife. The author shares from several years of experience of being in the pastorate. For a more recent work, see also, Frances Nordland, **The Unprivate Life of a Pastor's Wife,** Moody Press, 1972.

SHELLY, MARSHALL. **Well-Intentioned Dragons.** Vol.1. Waco, TX: Word Books, 1985.

This book is one in a series being produced by the editors of **Leadership** magazine. These books are extremely practical and helpful to those in the ministry.

TAYLOR, WILLIAM MACKERGO. **The Ministry of the Word.** Grand Rapids: Baker Book House, 1975.

Another outstanding classic book from the Lyman Beecher lectures on preaching. This book was out-of-print for many years.

TURNBULL, RALPH G. **A Minister's Obstacles.**
Westwood, N. J.: Fleming H. Revell Co., 1964.
A very helpful book dealing with the everyday challenges
that most minister's have to face. For another practical book,
see also, Lloyd M. Perry and Edward J. Lias, **A Manual of
Pastoral Problems and Procedures,** Baker Book House, 1962.

PASTORAL CARE AND COUNSELING

ADAMS, JAY EDWARD. **Competent to Counsel.** Nutley,
NJ: Presbyterian and Reformed Publishing Co., 1970.
This book traces all personalities problems to sin. While this
may be true in many cases, it is not true in every situation.
Adam's book still has some good things to contribute to pasto-
ral care and counseling.
BRISTER, C. W. **Pastoral Care in the Church.** New York:
Harper and Row, 1964.
A comprehensive outline of pastoral care recommended to
all who seek a deeper understanding of their role in the curing
of souls. For another helpful work in pastoral care, see also,
Wayne B. Oates and Andrew D. Lester, eds., **Pastoral Care in
Crucial Human Situations,** Judson Press, 1969. Both of these
works are helpful, but lack biblical foundations in areas.
CLINEBELL, HOWARD JOHN, JR. **Basic Types of Pasto-
ral Counseling.** Nashville: Abingdon Press, 1966.
This helpful book is a standard work in many colleges and
seminaries. It reveals the various kinds of counseling. Like
many books on counseling, it lacks a solid biblical foundation
in several areas. For a more biblical approach, see, Clyde M.
Narramore, **The Psychology of Counseling,** Zondervan Publishing House, 1960.
COLLINS, GARY R. **Christian Counseling: A Comprehensive Guide.** Waco, TX: Word Books, 1980.
A good overview of twenty-seven counseling issues. Lacks
biblical content. For another helpful work, see also, Wayne B.
Oates, **An Introduction to Pastoral Counseling,** Broadman
Press, 1959.

DUTY, GUY. **Divorce and Remarriage.** Minneapolis: Bethany Fellowship, 1967.

This is a good biblical approach to an explosive subject. Duty presents a compassionate and balanced study of divorce and remarriage. For another, helpful study, see also, John Murray, **Divorce,** Baker Book House, 1961.

GILBERT, MARVIN G. AND RAYMOND T. BROCK, eds. **The Holy Spirit and Counseling.** Peabody, MA: Hendrickson Publishers, 1986.

An important work that examines the biblical foundations of the Holy Spirit's dynamic as "Comforter" in the counseling process. Practical.

MACE, DAVID ROBERT, AND VERA MACE. **Marriage Enrichment in the Church.** Nashville: Broadman Press, 1976.

This book is a guide to help couples enhance their marriage relationship. For another helpful work, see also, William E. Hulme, **Pastoral Care of Families: Its Theology and Practice.** Abingdon Press, 1962.

MORRIS, JAMES KENNETH. **Marriage Counseling: A Manual for Ministers.** Englewood Cliffs, N. J.: Prentice-Hall, 1965.

A practical manual that covers the entire counseling process for couples in conflict. For premarital counseling, see also, James K. Morris, **Premarital Counseling: A Manual for Ministers,** Prentice-Hall, 1960.

HEALING

GORDON, A. J. **The Ministry of Healing.** Harrisburg, Penn.: Christian Publications, 1961.

Gordon points out various miracle healings that have taken place in all ages. For another helpful work, see also, A. B. Simpson, **The Gospel of Healing,** Christian Publications, 1915.

JETER, HUGH. **By His Stripes.** Springfield, MO.: Gospel Publishing House, 1977.

The classical Pentecostal case for healing as part of Christ's atonement. See also, Rita Bennett, **How to Pray for Inner Healing for Yourself and Others,** Fleming H. Revell Co., 1984.

TORREY, R. A. **Divine Healing.** Grand Rapids: Baker Book House, n.d.

A helpful systematic study on the topic of divine healing. For another practical work, see also, Andrew Murray, **Divine Healing,** Christian Literature Crusade, n. d.

TOURNIER, PAUL. **The Healing of Persons.** Translated by Edwin Hudson. New York: Harper and Row, 1965.

Tournier has several good works on counseling that are worth consulting. This book stresses the importance of healing in order to have a proper relationship with God. While Tournier is a good writer, his theology is weak. For another helpful work, see also, David Seamonds, **Healing for Damaged Emotions,** Victor Books, 1979.

Books on Devotional Literature

A good set of devotional books can restore the broken streams and put one in touch again with the living truth. In fact, one good book can deeply influence a person for life. Devotional reading is not an option for the minister, it is a must.

Our struggles and temptations are common to others who have served in the ministry. Their insights are of practical help to us in the fundamentals of daily life. Reading the experiences of others will help us to gain insights into the work of the ministry.

A good devotional book may be read over and over until we remember it; and, if we forget it, may again pick it up at our pleasure or at our leisure. The great advantage of rereading is that it gives one the true possession of the book. Besides, though the book does not change while it awaits us on the shelf, we keep changing.

The books listed in this section will deal with the minister's own personal Bible study and the personal life and experience of others. Several good volumes on prayer will be considered. This section will conclude with some helpful works on the Christian home.

PERSONAL BIBLE STUDY

JENSEN, IRVING LESTER. **Independent Bible Study.** Chicago: Moody Press, 1963.

Focuses on the inductive method of Bible study. A helpful work. For a more extensive work, see also, Lawrence O. Richards, **Creative Bible Study,** Zondervan Publishing House, 1971.

WALD, OLETTA. **Joy of Discovery.** Minneapolis: Bible Banner Press, n. d.

Wald knew how to study the Bible. This practical book will aid anybody in the joy of Bible study. For a more extensive work, see also, Lloyd M. Perry and Robert Duncan Culver, **How to Search the Scriptures,** Baker Book House, 1967.

PERSONAL LIFE AND EXPERIENCE

BUNYAN, JOHN. **The Pilgrims Progress.** Grand Rapids: Zondervan Publishing House, reprint.

A classic allegory of the Christian life by an excellent devotional writer. For another helpful work, see also, John Bunyan, **Grace Abounding to the Chief of Sinners.** New York: Oxford University Press, 1966.

DAYTON, EDWARD RISEDORPH, AND THEODORE WILHELM ENGSTROM. **Strategy for Living.** Glendale, CA: Regal Books, 1976.

These two authors have much to say about living a more effective Christian life. For another good work, see also, Victor R. Edman, **The Disciplines of Life,** Scripture Press, 1948.

GETZ, GENE A. **The Measure of a Man.** Glendale, CA: Regal Books, 1974.

A practical study on the teaching of the apostle Paul in relationship to leadership in the local church. For another helpful book, see also, John F. MacArthur, Jr., **Keys to Spiritual Growth,** Fleming H. Revell Co., 1976.

HOPKINS, EVAN HENRY. **The Law of Liberty in the Spiritual Life.** Fort Washington, Penn. Christian Literature Crusade, 1952.

This devotional classic should be obtained and read by every minister. For another good devotional classic, see also, William Law, **A Serious Call to a Devout and Holy Life,** Wm. B. Eerdmans Publishing Co., 1966.

MURRAY, ANDREW. **Abide in Christ.** Three Hills, Alberta: Prairie Book Room, n. d.

An excellent devotional study from a great writer on the Christian life. This author has written several other devotional books worth consulting. For another good devotional writer, see also, John C. Ryle, **Practical Religion,** Edited by J. I. Packer, James Clarke and Co., 1970.

STOTT, JOHN ROBERT WALMSEY. **Focus on Christ.** London: Wm. Collins Publishers, 1979.

These practical messages stress the importance of the centrality of Christ in the believer's life. For another helpful work, see also, Marion H. Nelson, **How to Know God's Will,** Moody Press, 1962.

SWINDOLL, CHARLES ROZELL. **Three Steps Forward, Two Steps Back: Persevering Through Pressure.** Nashville: Thomas Nelson Publishers, 1980.

Swindoll has written several excellent books on the Christian life. This work is outstanding. For another good devotional book, see also, Matthew Henry, **The Secret of Communion with God.** Fleming H. Revell Co., 1963.

TOURNIER, PAUL. **The Adventure of Life.** Translated by Edwin Hudson. New York: Harper and Row, 1965.

A helpful devotional study on finding fulfillment in the Christian life. For another good work, see also, Paul Tournier, **The Person Reborn,** Translated by Edwin Hudson, Harper and Row, 1966.

TOZER, AIDEN WILSON. **The Pursuit of God.** Harrisburg, Penn.: Christian Publications, 1948.

Tozer's devotional books are still in great demand. This work on the spiritual life is one of his best books. For another helpful work, see also, Aiden W. Tozer, **The Divine Conquest,** Fleming H. Revell Co., 1950.

(Note: There are a lot of good books on devotional literature that are not included in this section. I have just listed some of the basic volumes for the minister's library.)

PRAYER

BOUNDS, EDWARD MCKENDREE. **Power Through Prayer.** Grand Rapids: Zondervan Publishing House, 1965.

Every minister will want to read all of this author's devotional works. For another good devotional writer, see also, S. D. Gordon, **Quiet Talks on Prayer,** Fleming H. Revell Co., 1904.

FINNEY, CHARLES G. **Prevailing Prayer.** Grand Rapids: Kregel Publications, 1967.

A series of sermons on prayer. Finney discusses, prevailing prayer, confidence in prayer, praying always and prayer for the Holy Spirit. For another good book on prayer, see also, Arthur W. Pink, **Gleanings From Paul—Studies in the Prayers of the Apostle,** Moody Press, 1971.

MURRAY, ANDREW. **The Prayer Life, The Inner Chamber and the Deepest Secret of Pentecost.** Grand Rapids: Zondervan Publishing House, n. d.

This is one of the best books on prayer in print today. For another classic work, see also, Andrew Murray, **With Christ in the School of Prayer,** Fleming H. Revell Co., 1953.

————. **The Ministry of Intercession.** Westwood, N. J.: Fleming H. Revell Co., 1966.

One of the best books on intercessory prayer is this volume by Andrew Murray. Practical. For another good work on prayer, see also, Reuben A. Torrey, **How to Pray,** Fleming H. Revell Co., 1900.

STEDMAN, ROY C. **Jesus Teaches on Prayer.** Waco, TX: Word Books, 1975.

This is one of the better modern treatments on prayer and the Christian life. Stedman is a good expository preacher.
(Please note: The author has listed other helpful books on prayer under the Gospel of Matthew and John.)

CHRISTIAN HOME

ANDERSON, WAYNE J. **Design for Family Living.** Minneapolis: T. S. Denison and Co., 1964.

A helpful discussion on the needs of each member of the family. For another practical work on the family, see also, Wayne J. Anderson, **How to Explain Sex to Children,** T. D. Denison and Co., 1971.

BURKETT, LARRY, **What Husbands Wish Their Wives Knew About Money.** Wheaton, IL: Victor Books, 1977.

All of Burkett's books about money are worth consulting on a regular basis. For another excellent book on money, see also, George Fooshe, Jr., **You Can Be Financially Free,** Fleming H. Revell Co., 1976.

CHAPPELL, CLOVIS GILLHAM. **Home Folks.** Grand Rapids: Baker Book House, 1974.

Practical sermons on marriage and the home. Excellent. For another good series of sermons on marriage, see also, Clarence E. Macartney, **The Way of a Man With a Maid,** Baker Book House, 1974.

CHRISTENSON, LARRY. **The Christian Family.** Minneapolis: Bethany Fellowship, 1970.

An excellent guidebook for the Christian home. This is one of the best books on this subject. For another helpful work, see also, Gene A. Getz, **The Measure of a Family,** Regal Books, 1976.

DOBSON, JAMES. **Dare to Discipline.** Wheaton: Tyndale House Publishers, 1970.

This is one of the better books on the discipline of children. For another companion volume, see also, James Dobson, **Hide or Seek,** Fleming H. Revell Co., 1974.

————. **Straight Talk to Men and Their Wives.** Waco, TX: Word Books, 1980.

This practical work by Dr. Dobson focuses on the ministry of men to their families. It also includes some advice for wives and mothers. For another companion volume, see also, James Dobson, **What Wives Wish Their Husbands Knew About Women,** Tyndale House Publishers, 1975.

HENDRICKS, HOWARD GEORGE. **Heaven Help the Home.** Wheaton: Victor Books, 1973.

A very practical book on the home. Hendricks has some other writings on the family that are worth consulting. For another good work, see also, Ray C. Stedman, et al., **Family Life: God's View of Relationships,** Word Books, 1976.

KESSLER, JAY (comp.). **Parents and Teenagers.** Wheaton, IL.: Victor Books, 1974.

Here is some good practical advice from over fifty Christian leaders. Kessler compiled these selections from a wide variety of authorities. For another good work, see also, Jay Kessler, **Too Big to Spank,** Regal Books, 1978.

MACDONALD, GORDON. **The Effective Father.** Wheaton, IL: Tyndale House Publishers, 1977.

MacDonald uses biblical principles in this effective study of fatherhood. For another helpful study, see also, William Barclay, **Train Up a Child,** Westminster Press, 1960.

PETERSON, J. ALLAN (comp.). **The Marriage Affair.** Wheaton, IL: Tyndale House Publishers, 1971.

In these pages, more than seventy distinguished leaders discuss most of the vital issues of family living. Excellent. For another helpful work, see also, Howard E. (Tim) Timmons, **Maximum Marriage,** Fleming H. Revell Co., 1976.

SWINDOLL, CHARLES R. **You and Your Child.** Nashville: Thomas Nelson Publishers, 1977.

A helpful guidebook to rearing children effectively. For another excellent work, see also, James Dobson, **The Strong-Willed Child,** Tyndale House Publishers, 1983.

WHEAT, ED. **Love Life for Every Married Couple.** Grand Rapids: Zondervan Publishing House, 1980.

Another excellent book from the author of **Intended for Pleasure.** For another good book on marriage, see also, Chuck Swindoll, **Strike the Original Match,** Multnomah press, 1980.

WRIGHT, H. NORMAN. **Communication: Key to Your Marriage.** Glendale, CA: Regal Books, 1974.

This is an excellent book on the ways of communicating in a marriage. For another good work on marriage, see also, Chuck Swindoll, **Home, Where Life Makes Up Its Mind,** Multnomah Press, 1979.

————. **The Pillars of Marriage.** Glendale, CA: Regal Books, 1979.

Another good work from an experienced marriage counselor. For another good work, see also, Harry N. Wright, **In-Laws, Outlaws: Building Better Relationships,** Harvest House Publications, 1977. This author has other books that are worth consulting.

Books on Ecclesiastical Theology

This section will include volumes that deal with the mission and nature of the church. In addition, I will include books on public and private worship, along with works on the ceremonies and ordinances of the church and the conducting of weddings and funerals.

THE CHURCH

GANGEL, KENNETH O. **Leadership for Church Education.** Chicago: Moody Press, 1970.
Gangels points out some weaknesses of the church and how these deficiencies can be rectified. For another good work, see also, William J. Martin, **The Church in Mission,** Gospel Publishing House, 1986.
GETZ, GENE A. **Building Up One Another.** Wheaton, IL: Victor Books, 1976.
An excellent discussion on the "one another" passages in the Bible. For another good book, see also, Gene A. Getz, **Sharpening the Focus of the Church,** Moody Press, 1974.
LLOYD-JONES, DAVID MARTYN. **The Basis of Christian Unity.** Grand Rapids: Wm. B. Eerdmans Publishing Co., 1963.
A brief, but helpful volume on the scriptural basis for Christian unity. For another helpful work, see also, Rienk B. Kuiper, **The Glorious Body of Christ,** Wm. B. Eerdmans Publishing Co., 1955.
MORGAN, GEORGE CAMPBELL. **Peter and the Church.** Grand Rapids: Baker Book House, 1974.
This scriptural study on the nature of the church is extremely valuable. For a more modern study, see also, Alfred E. Kuen, **I Will Build My Church.** Moody Press, 1971.
PERRY, LLOYD MERLE, **Getting the Church on Target.** Chicago: Moody Press, 1977.
Perry shares his rich experiences about the church's life and function. For another helpful work, see also, Howard Snyder, **The Problem of Wineskins: Church Structure in a Technological Age,** Inter Varsity Press, 1975.

RYLE, JOHN CHARLES. **Warnings to the Churches.** London: Banner of Truth Trust, 1967.

Ryle's writings are extremely practical. This work on ecclesiology is very helpful in pointing out some dangers in many churches.

PUBLIC WORSHIP

GIBBS, ALFRED P. **Worship—The Christian's Highest Occupation.** Kansas City, Kansas: Walternick Publishers, n. d.

This work abounds with practical material on the biblical teaching of worship. For another helpful work, see also, Robert G. Rayburn, **O Come, Let Us Worship: Corporate Worship in the Evangelical Church,** Baker Book House, 1980.

MARTIN, RALPH PHILIP. **Worship in the Early Church.** Westwood, N. J.: Fleming H. Revell Co., 1964.

A helpful, historical study on Christian worship. This book has a Baptist slant. For another good work, see also, Roger T. Beckwith and Wilfrid Stott, **This is the Day: The Biblical Doctrine of the Christian Sunday in Its Jewish and Christian Setting,** Attic Press, 1978.

CEREMONIES AND ORDINANCES

CHRISTENSEN, JAMES L. **The Minister's Service Handbook.** Westwood, N. J.: Fleming H. Revell Co., 1960.

This handbook will aid any minister in the performance of various services. For another similar work, see also, Samuel W. Hutton, **Minister's Service Manual,** Baker Book House, 1965.

CRISWELL, WALLIE AMOS. **Criswell's Guidebook For Pastors.** Nashville: Broadman Press, 1980.

A wealth of practical information on the pastorate by a respected pastor. This is a comprehensive work covering several areas of Ecclesiastical Theology. Evangelical.

PICTHORN, WILLIAM E. (comp.) **Minister's Manual.** 3 vols. Springfield, MO.: Gospel Publishing House, 1965.

This practical work includes, services for special occasions, services for weddings and funerals and services for ministers and workers. For another excellent work, see also, James L. Christensen, **The Complete Handbook For Ministers: A Collection of Traditional and Contemporary Services,** Baker Book House, 1985.

BAPTISM

HOWARD, JAMES KERI. **New Testament Baptism.** London: Pickering and Inglis, 1970.
An excellent New Testament study on water baptism. The author concludes with the teaching that immersion was the "normal mode." For another helpful study, see also, Alexander Carson, **Baptism, Its Mode and Its Subjects,** Baker Book House, 1957.

LORD'S SUPPER

HENRY, MATTHEW. **The Communicant's Companion; or, Instructions for the Right Receiving of the Lord's Supper.** Joplin, MO.: College Press, 1969.
An extremely practical treatise on the Lord's Supper. For another good work, see also, Alfred P. Gibbs, **The Lord's Supper,** Walterick Publishers, 1963.

MURRAY, ANDREW. **The Lord's Table.** Fort Washington, Penn.: Christian Literature Crusade, 1962.
This devotional work by Murray is excellent. For another excellent reprint, see also, Alexander Whyte, **In Remembrance of Me,** Baker Book House, 1970.

JEREMIAS, JOACHIM. **The Eucharistic Words of Jesus.** Translated by Arnold Ehrhardt. Oxford: Basil Blackwell, 1955.
A good historical study on the Lord's supper. Unfortunately, some of the author's theology cannot be accepted by the evangelical.

MARRIAGE

CHRISTENSEN, JAMES L. **The Minister's Marriage Handbook.** Westwood, N. J.: Fleming H. Revell Co., 1966.
Christensen's book on weddings is one of the most comprehensive works available. For another helpful work, see also, Samuel W. Hutton, **Minister's Marriage Manual.** Baker Book House, 1968.

FUNERALS

CHRISTENSEN, JAMES L. **Funeral Services.** Westwood: N. J.: Fleming H. Revell Co., 1959.
A complete work on everything that a minister needs to know regarding the funeral service. For another helpful work, see also, Andrew Blackwood, **The Funeral,** Westminster Press, 1942.
CRISWELL, WALLIE AMOS. **Our Home in Heaven.** Grand Rapids: Zondervan Publishing House, 1965.
This practical book contains several biblical passages for comforting the bereaved. In addition, it has some sermon ideas and poems. Evangelical. For another helpful work, see also, Herbert Lockyer, **The Funeral Source Book,** Zondervan Publishing House, 1967.

Books on Missions and Evangelism

The primary mission of the Church of Jesus Christ on earth is to be a witness for Him. Evangelism is the primary task of telling the good news of Jesus to every man with a view to his conversion. Beyond this, evangelism also includes presenting every believer mature in Jesus Christ. To be most effective in fulfilling the commission of Christ, one should have a knowledge of some good books on missions and evangelism.

In this section, I will be recommending books on missions, evangelism, church growth, church leadership and administration, church management, stewardship, church music and church ministries. This is a very important part of this book, so study these selections carefully.

MISSIONS

ALLEN, ROLAND. **Missionary Methods: St. Paul's or Ours?** Grand Rapids: Wm. B. Eerdmans Publishing Co., 1962.

Even though this work was first published in 1912, it is still helpful. For another practical study, see also, Roland Allen, **The Spontaneous Expansion of the Church and the Causes Which Hinder It.** Wm. B. Eerdmans Publishing Co., 1962.

BEYERHAUS, PETER AND HENRY LEFEVER. **The Responsible Church and the Foreign Mission.** Grand Rapids: Wm. B. Eerdmans Publishing Co., 1964.

A good balanced work on the responsibility of the local church to missions and the foreign missions responsibility to the local church. For a good theology on missions see also, Harry Boer, **Pentecost and Missions,** Wm. B. Eerdmans Publishing Co., 1961.

CHAMBERS, OSWALD. **So Send I You.** Philadelphia: Christian Literature Crusade, 1960.

From one of the greatest missionary statesman of all time. A challenging book. For another challenging work, see also, Robert H. Glover, **The Bible Basis of Missions,** Moody Press, 1964.

KANE, J. HERBERT. **A Concise History of the Christian**

World Mission: A Panoramic View of Missions from Pentecost to Present. Grand Rapids: Baker Book House, 1978.

A standard text on the history and current status of Christian missions throughout the world. For another helpful study, see also, J. Herbert Kane, **Christian Missions in Biblical Perspective,** Baker Book House, 1976.

PETERS, GEORGE W. **A Biblical Theology of Missions.** Chicago: Moody Press, 1973.

This modern theology on missions is based on sound biblical principles. For another good work, see also, Harold Lindsell, **An Evangelical Theology of Missions,** Zondervan Publishing House, 1970.

POMERVILLE, PAUL A. **The Third Force in Missions.** Peabody, MA.: Hendrickson Publishers, 1986.

This volume is an incisive evaluation of the contribution of the Pentecostal movement to contemporary mission theology. In this book, the reader will be challenged to recognize the indispensable role of the Holy Spirit as a power-for-mission.

STOTT, JOHN ROBERT WALMSEY. **Christian Mission in the Modern World.** Downers Grove, IL: Inter Varsity Press, 1975.

A vital contemporary study of missions in our world. For another helpful work, see also, Melvin L. Hodges, **A Guide to Church Planting,** Moody Press, 1974.

EVANGELISM

COLEMAN, ROBERT E. **The Master Plan of Evangelism.** Westwood, N. J.: Fleming H. Revell Co., 1964.

Every minister needs to read this book several times. Excellent. For another good work, see also, George W. Peters, **Saturation Evangelism,** Zondervan Publishing House, 1970.

EDWARDS, GENE. **How to Have a Soul Winning Church.** Springfield, MO.: Gospel Publishing House, 1963.

A very practical book on personal evangelism and the local church. For a practical work on street evangelism, see, Jonathan Gainsbrugh, **Take Him to the Streets,** Custom Graphics, 1979.

GETZ, GENE A. **Loving One Another.** Wheaton, IL: Victor Books, 1979.   This important book clears up several misconceptions about personal evangelism. For another helpful work, see also, Edward M. B. Green, **Evangelism in the Early Church,** Wm. B. Eerdmans Publishing Co., 1970.

LITTLE, PAUL. **How to Give Away Your Faith.** Downers Grove, IL: Inter Varsity, 1966.
A practical training tool for witnessing and for training others. An excellent guide for every believer that wants to be an effective witness for Christ. For a more extensive book, see also, D. James Kennedy, **Evangelism Explosion,** Tyndale House Publishers, 1977.

LLOYD-JONES, DAVID MARTYN. **Evangelistic Sermons.** Grand Rapids: Baker Book House, 1985.
Here are twenty-one sermons from a master evangelistic preacher. For another helpful work, see also, Faris D. Whitesell, **Sixty-five Ways to Give an Evangelistic Invitation,** Zondervan Publishing House, 1955.

SPURGEON, CHARLES HADDON. **The Soul Winner.** Condensed and edited by David Otis Fuller. 2d ed. Grand Rapids: Zondervan Publishing House, 1948.
A valuable, classic work that was first published in 1895. For another good work, see also, Elmer L. Towns, **Evangelize Through Christian Education,** Evangelical Teacher Training Association, 1970.

STOTT, JOHN ROBERT WALMSEY. **Our Guilty Silence: The Church, the Gospel, and the World.** Grand Rapids: Wm. B. Eerdmans Publishing Co., 1969.
This is a study challenging the church to stay with its primary mission of evangelism instead of debate reform and social services. For another helpful tool of evangelism, see also, Arthur G. McPhee, **Friendship Evangelism,** Zondervan Publishing House, 1978.

CHURCH GROWTH

ARN, WINFIELD C. AND CHARLES ARN. **Master's Plan for Making Disciples.** Pasadena, CA: Church Growth Press, 1982.

Two church growth authorities team up and present a very helpful study on discipleship. For another helpful work, see also, Gene A. Getz, **The Measure of a Church,** Regal Books, 1979.

HAMILTON, MICHAEL. **God's Plan for the Church-Growth.** Springfield, MO.: Gospel Publishing House, 1980.

A brief, but practical little book on church growth. Pentecostal/Charismatic. For a larger work, see, Elmer Towns, **The Complete Book of Church Growth,** Tyndale House, 1982.

MCGAVERAN, DONALD, AND WINFIELD C. ARN. **How to Grow a Church.** Glendale, CA: Regal Books, 1973.

This is one of the earlier books on church growth. It is still worth consulting. For another good work, see also, Donald McGaveran and Winfield C. Arn, **Ten Steps for Church Growth,** Harper and Row Publishers, 1977.

MCGAVRAN, DONALD; ARN, CHARLES; ARN, WIN. **Growth, A New Vision for the Sunday School.** Pasadena, CA: Church Growth Press, 1980.

One of the better books on church growth and the Sunday school. This work is very practical. For another helpful book, see also, Donald A. McGavran, **Understanding Church Growth,** Wm. B. Eerdmans Publishing Co., 1980.

TILLAPAUGH, FRANK. **The Church Unleased.** Ventura, Calif.: Regal, 1982.

An excellent book showing the various ways a church can free its members to minister effectively in the world. For another helpful work, see also, Lyle E. Shaller, **Activating the Passive Church,** Abingdon, 1983. This author has several good books on church growth that are worth consulting.

WAGNER, C. PETER. **Your Church Can Be Healthy.** Nashville: Abingdon Press, 1979.

This book gives an excellent analysis of the symptoms and causes of eight common diseases in American churches.

WAGNER, C. PETER. **Your Church Can Grow: Seven Vital Signs of a Healthy Church.** Glendale, Calif.: Regal Book, 1976.

This work can be a helpful tool in diagnosing effectiveness in the local congregation. For another practical book, see also, C. Peter Wagner, **Leading Your Church to Growth,** Regal Books, 1983.

CHURCH LEADERSHIP AND ADMINISTRATION

BEEBE, WALLY. **All About the Second Man.** Murfreesboro, Tenn.: Sword of the Lord Publishers, 1971.

A very helpful work on the role of an associate pastor. This is one of the few books written on this important subject.

DAYTON, EDWARD RISEDORPH, AND THEODORE WILHELM ENGSTROM. **Strategy for Leadership.** Old Tappen, NJ: Fleming H. Revell Company, 1979.

These two authors are outstanding authorities in the field of church management and leadership. Excellent. For another good work, see also, Theodore W. Engstrom and Edward R. Dayton, **The Christian Executive,** Word Books, 1979.

DRESSELHAUS, RICHARD L. **The Deacon and His Ministry.** Springfield, MO.: Gospel Publishing House, 1977.

This is one of the few books written on the ministry of a deacon in a local church. A very practical guide.

DRUCKER, PETER FERDINAND. **The Effective Executive.** New York: Harper and Row, 1967.

Drucker has some very helpful books on administration, management and leadership. This book is an important contribution.

GERIG, DONALD. **Leadership in Crises.** Glendale, CA: Regal Books, 1981.

A positive and stimulating book examining the crises in leadership. For another helpful work, see also, LeRoy Eims, **Be the Leader You Were Meant to Be: What the Bible Says About Leadership,** Victor Books, 1975.

RICHARDS, LAWRENCE O., AND CLYDE

HOELDTKE. **A Theology of Church Leadership.** Grand Rapids: Zondervan Publishing House, 1980.

This serious study of church leadership develops the concept of leadership servanthood and stresses people-oriented rather than project-oriented outreach. Excellent. For another good work, see also, Lawrence O. Richards and Gib Martin, **A Theology of Personal Ministry,** Zondervan Publishing House, 1984.

SCHULLER, ROBERT HAROLD. **Your Church Has Real Possibilities!** Glendale, CA: Regal Books, 1975.

This book contains some practical guidelines on successful leadership and church growth. For another very practical book on leadership, see also, Charles E. Jones, **Life is Tremendous,** Tyndale House Publishers, 1968.

CHURCH MANAGEMENT

BAUGHEN, MICHAEL. **The Moses Principle: Leadership and the Venture of Faith.** Wheaton, IL: Harold Shaw Publishers, 1979.

In this important book, Baughen discusses the skills which made Moses a man of God and an outstanding leader of the nation of Israel.

DRUCKER, PETER FERDINAND. **Managing for Results.** New York: Harper and Row, 1964.

A helpful work in the field of management strategy and decision making. For a more evangelical approach, see also, Theodore W. Engstrom, **The Making of a Christian Leader,** Zondervan Publishing House, 1976.

HAMMER, RICHARD R. **Pastor Church & Law.** Springfield, MO.: Gospel Publishing House, 1983.

This book represents the best comprehensive study of American church law in recent history. Excellent. A supplement can now be purchased from Gospel Publishing House. For another important book for the minister, see also, General Henry M. Robert, **Robert's Rules of Order,** Revised, Morrow Quill Paperbacks, 1979.

HOLCK, MANFRED. **Making It on a Pastor's Pay.** Nashville: Abingdon Press, 1974.

This author has several helpful books on church management. In this work, Holck gives many practical suggestions to leaders in establishing a pastor's salary. For another helpful book on church management, see also, Raymond W. McLaughlin, **Communication for the Church,** Zondervan Publishing House, 1968.

HYLES, JACK. **The Hyles Church Manual.** Murfreesboro, Tenn.: Sword of the Lord Publishers, 1968.

A very practical manual covering nearly every area of church management by a successful Baptist pastor. For another helpful work on the smaller church, see also, Harold Longenecker, **The Village Church: Its Pastor and Program,** Moody Press, 1961.

SWEET, HERMAN J. **The Multiple Staff in the Local Church.** Philadelphia: Westminster Press, 1963.

A helpful book for pastors who want to be more effective in their staff relationships. For another helpful work, see also, Lyle E. Shaller, **The Multiple Staff and the Larger Church,** Abingdon Press, 1980.

STEWARDSHIP

DOLLAR, TRUMAN. **How To Carry Out God's Stewardship Plan.** Nashville: Thomas Nelson Publishers, 1974.

An excellent book that spells out in clear detail the step-by-step planning and execution of the stewardship ministry of the local church. For other books on stewardship, see comments under the Christian home.

HOLCK, MANFRED, JR. **Money and Your Church: How to Raise More How to Manage It Better.** Connecticut: Keats Publishing, 1974.

A very practical book in budgeting and accounting for the local church. For another helpful book, see also, David Walter Thompson, **How to Increase Memorial Giving,** Fleming H. Revell Co., 1963.

OLFORD, STEPHEN. **The Grace of Giving.** Grand Rapids: Zondervan Publishing House, 1972.
Contains seven practical messages on stewardship. Excellent. For another helpful work, see also, George A. E. Salstrand, **The Grace of Giving,** Baker Book House, 1964.

CHURCH MUSIC

JOHANSSON, CALVIN M. **Music & Ministry.** Peabody, MA.: Hendrickson Publishers, 1985.
This is one of the most comprehensive books in the area of church music. Excellent. For another helpful work, see also, Lynn W. Thayer, **The Church Music Handbook,** Zondervan Publishing House, 1971.
OSBECK, KENNETH W. **101 Hymn Stories.** Grand Rapids: Kregel Publications, 1981.
Excellent for devotional readings, sermon illustrations and bulletin inserts. For another helpful book, see also, Kenneth W. Osbeck, **101 More Hymn Stories,** Kregel Publications, 1984.

CHURCH MINISTRIES

HUGEN, MELVIN D. **The Church's Ministry to the Older Unmarried.** Grand Rapids: Wm. B. Eerdmans Publishing Co., 1960.
This book meets an important need in our growing older generation. For another helpful book, see also, Nevin C. Hatner, **The Educational Work of the Church,** Abingdon-Cokesbury Press, 1952.
WILKERSON, DAVID. **The Cross and The Switchblade.** New York: B. Geiss Associates, 1963.
An excellent book on Wilkerson's fight against teen-age problems. For another good work, see also, David Wilkerson and Don Wilkerson, **The Gutter and the Ghetto.** Word Books, 1969.

Books on Christian Education

Christian education must be based on biblical principles. In this section, several books on the Christian education ministry will be covered, including administration and organization, leadership training, curriculum, the relation of Christian education to evangelism and discipleship, staffing needs, methodology, and the impact of the Christian education ministry on family life.

Pastors need to realize that Christian education is the heart of the local church. It exists to carry out two important functions: evangelism (to make disciples) and edification (to nurture disciples and equip them for ministry) (Matt. 28: 19–20; Eph. 4:10–12). Evangelical Christian education should include the process of planning and guiding the experiences of the learners so that they are confronted with the central realities of God and His redemptive acts through Jesus Christ in an atmosphere of loving acceptance made possible by the atonement. Pastors need to have access to a wide range of books to carry out this philosophy of Christian education.

GENERAL REFERENCE BOOKS

BYRNE, HERBERT W. **A Christian Approach to Education.** Grand Rapids: Zondervan Publishing House, 1961.

Byrne presents a biblical approach to Christian education. An excellent study. For another good work, see also, Herbert W. Byrne, **Improving Church Education,** Religious Education Press, 1979.

EAVEY, CHARLES BENTON. **History of Christian Education.** Chicago: Moody Press, 1964.

One of the most thorough works on the history of Christian education. For another helpful study, see also, Elmer L. Towns, ed., **A History of Religious Educators,** Baker Book House, 1975.

EDGE, FINDLEY BARTOW. **A Quest for Vitality in Religion: A Theological Approach to Religious Education.** Nashville: Broadman Press, 1963.

Edge pleads for evangelicals to get back to the biblical approach to Christian education. Excellent. For another good work, see also, Lawrence O. Richards, **A Theology of Christian Education,** Zondervan Publishing House, 1975.

LEBAR, LOIS EMOGENE. **Education That Is Christian.** Westwood, N.J.: Fleming H. Revell Co., 1958.

Dr. Lebar's books on Christian education are excellent. In this book, the author gives a biblical philosophy of Christian education. For another good book, see also, Lois E. LeBar, **Focus on People in Church Education,** Fleming H. Revell Co., 1968.

ADMINISTRATION

BYRNE, HERBERT W. **Christian Education for the Local Church.** Grand Rapids: Zondervan Publishing House, 1963.

A very helpful volume on administering the Christian education program in the local church. For another good work, see also, Robert K. Bower, **Administering Christian Education: Principles of Administration for Ministers and Christian Leaders,** Wm. B. Eerdmans Publishing Co., 1964.

HYLES, JACK. **The Hyles Sunday School Manual.** Murfreesboro, Tenn.: Sword of the Lord Publishers, 1969.

The best way to describe this helpful guidebook on the Sunday school is practical. A very comprehensive work on this important area of the local church. For another very practical work, see also, Guy P. Leavett, **Superintend with Success,** Standard Publishing Co., 1960.

MCMICHAEL, BETTY. **The Library and Resource Center in Christian Education.** Chicago: Moody Press, 1977.

This is one of the best works in print on the church library. Practical and helpful.

PERSON, PETER P. **The Minister in Christian Education.** Grand Rapids: Baker Book House, 1960.

A helpful book showing the pastor's role in Christian education. For another basic work on Christian education, see also, Peter P. Person, **Introduction to Christian Education,** Baker Book House, 1960.

LEADERSHIP TRAINING

GREGORY, JOHN MILTON. **The Seven Laws of Teaching.**
Owatonna, MN: Pillsbury Press, 1976.

A classic work on what the author calls, **The Seven Laws of
Teaching.** For another very helpful work on teaching, see also,
Roy B. Zuck, **The Holy Spirit in Your Teaching,** Scripture
Press Publications, 1963.

Leadership Preparation Textbooks. Wheaton: Evangelical
Teacher Training Association, 1968.

These are some of the best teaching training booklets available. Here are fourteen booklets loaded with practical instruction for training lay people in the local church. Excellent.

PALMER, JOHN M. **Equipping for Ministry.** Springfield,
MO.: Gospel Publishing House, 1985.

A helpful work designed to help lay people discover their
ministry potential. For another good work, see also, Billie
Davis, **Teaching to Meet Crises Needs,** Gospel Publishing
House, 1984.

RICHARDS, LAWRENCE O., ed. **The Key to Sunday
School Achievement.** Chicago: Moody Press, 1965.

Richards is an outstanding Christian educator. This work
abounds with practical information on Sunday school achievement and training.

AGE-LEVEL DEPARTMENTS

GETZ, GENE A. **The Vacation Bible School in the Local
Church.** Chicago: Moody Press, 1962.

This is one of the best books in print on the vacation Bible
school. Many things have changed since this book was written,
but it is still helpful.

IRVING, ROY G. AND ROY B. ZUCK, eds. **Youth and the
Church: A Survey of the Church's Ministry to Youth.** Chicago:
Moody Press, 1967.

A practical work that covers every area of youth ministry.

For a more recent book, see also, Roy B. Zuck and Warren S. Benson, **Youth Education in the Church,** Moody Press, 1978.

LEBAR, LOIS EMOGENE. **Children in the Bible School: The How of Christian Education.** Westwood, N.J.: Fleming H. Revell Co., 1952.

An extremely practical book on working with children. For another good work on children, see also, Lois E. LeBar, **Church Time for Four's and Five's,** Scripture Press, 1961.

RICHARDS, LAWRENCE O. **A Theology of Children's Ministry.** Grand Rapids: Zondervan Publishing House, 1983.

This excellent work contains sound biblical theology on developing an effective ministry to children. For another helpful book, see also, Roy B. Zuck and Robert E. Clark, **Childhood Education in the Church,** Moody Press, 1981.

—————. **Youth Ministry Its Renewal in the Local Church.** Grand Rapids: Zondervan Publishing House, 1984.

This is one of the best recent works on youth ministry in the local church. For another helpful work, see also, Elmer Towns, **Successful Youth Work,** Regal Books, 1966.

TOWNS, ELMER L. **Ministering to the Young Single Adult.** Grand Rapids: Baker Book House, 1967.

A very helpful book on single adult ministry. This work will guide the user in exploring many questions confronting the church and the young single adult.

ZUCK, ROY B., AND GENE A. GETZ, eds. **Adult Education in the Church.** Chicago: Moody Press, 1970.

One of the best books on adult ministry in the church. For a smaller work, see also, Lawrence O. Richards, **You and Adults,** Moody Press, 1974.

—————. **Christian Youth, an In-Depth Study.** Chicago: Moody Press, 1968.

An extremely informative study of the various aspects of youth needs. This work contains the results of a survey of 3,000 teen-agers.

METHODOLOGY

BARRETT, ETHEL. **Story-Telling—It's Easy!** Los Angeles: Cowman Publications, 1960.

All pastors would do well to read this book. It would help in telling Bible stories from the pulpit more effectively. Barrett is the best authority on story-telling.

EDGE, FINDLEY BARTOW. **Teaching for Results.** Nashville: Broadman, 1956.

An excellent book on Christian teaching. For another good work, see also, Findley B. Edge, **Helping the Teacher,** Broadman Press, 1959.

GETZ, GENE A. **Audio-Visual Media in Christian Education.** Chicago: Moody Press, 1972.

This is the most complete textbook on religious audio-visual education. An extremely practical volume.

GANGEL, KENNETH O. **Understanding Teaching.** Wheaton: Evangelical Teacher Training Association, 1968.

A practical work that is helpful for use by superintendents in teacher's training. For another good book on methodology, see also, Kenneth O. Gangel, **24 Ways to Improve Your Teaching,** Victor Books, 1974.

LEAVITT, GUY P. **Teach with Success.** Cincinatti: Standard Publishing Co., 1956.

This is a self-teaching manual that will be of great help to all Sunday school teachers in the local church. Excellent.

RICHARDS, LAWRENCE O. **Creative Bible Teaching.** Chicago: Moody Press, 1970.

A must book for all evangelical pastors that wish to teach the Bible more creatively. This work will also be helpful to layman. For another good work, see also, Lawrence O. Richards, **You The Teacher,** Moody Press, 1972.

Section Nine

Books on Church History

On one occasion, Paul prayed that believers may comprehend "with all the saints what is the breadth and length and height and depth, and to know the love of Christ . . ." (Ephesians 3:18, 19). Our Christian heritage includes men and movements, institutions and ideas from different periods of church history. It is important for ministers to have good books on this history to fully appreciate this God-given heritage.

This section will not be extensive. It will list recommendations that have stood the test of time in the general field of church history. The final part of this section will include books on the various denominations and significant religious movements.

GENERAL REFERENCE BOOKS
CREEDS AND CONFESSIONS

SCHAFF, PHILLIP. **The Creeds of Christendom.** 6th ed. Revised and enlarged. 3 vols. Grand Rapids: Baker Book House, n. d.

A classic work on the history of the creeds and provides an appraisal of each. For another helpful book, see also, Charles Hodge, **The Confession of Faith,** Banner of Truth Trust, 1961.

CHURCH HISTORY

BRUCE, FREDERICK FYVIE. **The Spreading Flame.** Advance of Christianity through the Centuries. Grand Rapids: Wm. B. Eerdmans Publishing Co., 1958.

Bruce shows the progress of Christianity to the conversion of the English. For another helpful work, see also, Henry Chadwick, **The Early Church,** Pelican History of the Church, Wm. B. Eerdmans Publishing Co., 1968.

CROSS, FRANK LESLIE, ed. **The Oxford Dictionary of the Christian Church.** Oxford: Clarendon Press, 1958.

A helpful dictionary containing biographical, theological, and ecclesiastical articles. For another helpful work, see also,

Edwin S. Gaustad, **Historical Atlas of Religion in America,** New and Revised ed., Harper and Row, 1977.

D'AUBIGNE, JEAN HENRI MERLE. **The Reformation in England.** Edited by S. M. Houghton. 2 vols. London: Banner of Truth Trust, 1962–63.

D'Aubigne is the foremost and most inspirational writer on the reformation. This author has some other books on the reformation that are worth consulting. For another inspirational work, see also, Roland H. Bainton, **Here I Stand: A Life of Luther,** Abingdon Press, 1951.

Eerdmans' Handbook to the History of Christianity. Edited by T. Dowley. Grand Rapids: Wm. B. Eerdmans Publishing Co., 1977.

A practical volume pertaining to the history of the Christian church. For a more extensive study, see also, Kenneth S. Latourette, **A History of the Expansion of Christianity,** 7 vols., Zondervan Publishing House, 1971.

Foxes Book of Martyrs. Edited by William Byron Forbush. New York: Holt, Rinehart and Winston, 1926.

This is an abridgement of John Fox's book of Christian martyrs. A classic work on the lives, suffering and deaths of early Christian and Protestant martyrs. For a more extensive study, get the unabridged edition.

ESTEP, WILLIAM R. **The Anabaptist Story.** Nashville: Broadman Press, 1963.

An excellent presentation of the Anabaptists and how they influenced the growth of the free church movement in Europe.

NEAL, DANIEL. **The History of the Puritans; . . .** 3 vols. Minneapolis: Klock and Klock Christian Publishers, 1979.

This is the best known and most valuable work on the history of the Puritans. It covers the period from the Reformation to 1689. For another helpful work, see also, Elgin Moyer, **Wycliffe Biographical Dictionary of the Church,** Moody Press, 1982.

SCHAFF, PHILLIP. **History of the Christian Church.** 8 vols. Grand Rapids: Wm. B. Eerdmans Publishing Co., 1960.

One of the best works on the complete history of the Christian church in existence. Schaff has other books on church history that are worth consulting.

DENOMINATIONS

GAUSTED, EDWIN SCOTT. **Historical Atlas of Religion in America.** New and revised. ed. New York: Harper and Row, 1977.

An excellent handbook of all the major religious bodies in America. For another helpful work, see also, Clifton E. Olmstead, **History of Religion in the United States,** Prentice Hall, 1960.

PENTECOSTAL AND CHARISMATIC MOVEMENT

BURGESS, STANLEY M. **Dictionary of the American Pentecostal and Charismatic Movements.** Grand Rapids: Zondervan Publishing House, to be published.

This new work is to be published in 1988. The dictionary will contain articles on the books of the Bible, theological topics such as the person and work of the Holy Spirit, and history of the charismatic movement and prominent worldwide Pentecostal figures. Since no other resource of this nature is presently available, pastors, teachers, and Bible students should profit from the wealth of information it will contain. Other contributors have been selected largely from within the ranks of the Pentecostal and charismatic movements. For another informative study on the Pentecostal/Charismatic movement, see also, Walter J. Hollenweger, **The Pentecostals: The Charismatic Movement in the Churches,** Translated by R. A. Wilson, Augsburg Publishing House, 1972.

Books on Comparative Religions

Christianity is not to be viewed as just another of the religions of the world nor is it to be confused with any sect or cult. The historic Christian position is being questioned as never before by sects, cults and world religions.

The books in this last section will show where these non-Christian religions fall short of Christianity and give advice about how to convert these adherents to the evangelical message. All of the authors that are recommended believe and practice the historical Judeo-Christian faith.

SECTS AND CULTS

ENROTH, RONALD. **The Lure of the Cults.** Chappaqua, New York: Christian Herald Books, 1979.

An excellent book on the sensationalism that is propagated by the cults. For another helpful work, see also, Anthony A. Hoekema, **The Four Major Cults,** Wm. B. Eerdmans Publishing Co., 1963.

GERSTNER, JOHN H. **Theology of the Major Sects.** Grand Rapids: Baker Book House, 1960.

This is a practical work that exposes the false teaching of the modern sects. One of the few works written extensively on the sects.

MARTIN, WALTER RALSTON. **The Kingdom of the Cults.** Grand Rapids: Zondervan Publishing House, 1965.

Dr. Martin is one of the greatest authorities on the cults and the occult. Excellent. For another very helpful work, see also, Walter R. Martin, **The Kingdom of the Occult,** Vision House, 1974.

WORLD RELIGIONS

Eerdman's Handbook to the World's Religions. Grand Rapids: Wm. B. Eerdmans Publishing Co., 1982.

A comprehensive introduction to the world's religions from ancient Egypt, Greece, and Rome, to present day primal religions and the great religions—Hinduism, Buddhism, Judaism, Islam, and Christianity. Excellent. For a good older work, see also, Howard F. Vos, ed., **Religions in a Changing World,** Rev. ed., Moody Press, 1959.

Bibliography

BARBER, CYRIL J. **The Minister's Library.** 2 vols. Chicago: Moody Press, 1985–86.

BROOKMAN, DAVID W. **Basic Books for the Minister's Library.** Green Lane, Penn.: Northeast Bible Institute, 1971.

CHILDS, BREVARD S. **Old Testament Books for Pastor and Teacher.** Philadelphia: The Westminster Press, 1977.

DANKER, FREDERICK W. **Multipurpose Tools for Bible Study.** 2d rev. ed. St. Louis: Concordia Publishing House, 1966.

Essential Books for a Pastor's Library. Edited by the faculty of Union Theological Seminary. Richmond, VA.: Union Theological Seminary, 1968.

FEE, GORDON D. AND DOUGLAS STUART. **How to Read the Bible for All Its Worth.** Grand Rapids: Zondervan Publishing House, 1982.

JANNEY, JOHN. **Basic Books for Bible Study.** Wilmington, Del.: Sovereign Grace Publishers, n. d.

KELLY, BALMER H. AND DONALD G. MILLER. **Tools For Bible Study.** Richmond: John Knox Press, 1957.

KERR, RONN. **Directory of Bible Resources: A Comprehensive Guide to Tools for Bible Study.** Nashville: Thomas Nelson Publishers, 1983.

MCPHAIL, DAVID. **A Basic Bibliography for Ministers.** New York: Union Theological Seminary, 1960.

MERCHANT, HARISH D. **Encounter With Books.** Illinois: Inter-Varsity Press, 1970.

Recommended Basic Books for the Minister's Library. Edited by a faculty committee of Central Bible College. Springfield, MO.: Central Bible College, n. d.

SCHOLER, DAVID M. **A Basic Bibliographic Guide for New Testament Exegesis.** Grand Rapids: Wm. B. Eerdmans Publishing Co., 1973.

SMITH, JAY J. **Minister's Library Handbook.** Massachusetts: W. A. Wilde Company, 1958.

SMITH, WILBER M. **A Treasury of Books for Bible Study.** Massachusetts: W. A. Wilde Company, 1951.

————. **Chats from a Minister's Library.** Massachusetts: W. A. Wilde Company, 1951.

————. **Profitable Bible Study.** Massachusetts: W. A. Wilde Company, 1963.

————. **The Minister in His Study.** Chicago: Moody Press, 1973.

SPURGEON, CHARLES HADDON. **Commenting and Commentaries.** London: Banner of Truth Trust, 1969.

WIERSBE, WARREN W. **A Basic Library for Bible Students.** Grand Rapids: Baker Book House, 1981.

ZUCK, ROY B. **Bibliography for Old Testament Exegesis and Exposition.** Third Revised Edition. Dallas, TX.: Dallas Theological Seminary, 1975.

Author Index

Tenney, M. C., 8, 63, 82, 96, 115, 116, 135
Terry, M. S., 11
Thayer, J. H., 66
Thayer, L. W., 190
Thiele, E. R., 42
Thiessen, H. C., 122
Thiessen, J. C., 148
Thomas, D., 45, 49
Thomas, J. D., 144
Thomas, W. H. G., 25, 28, 73, 75, 80, 85, 89, 102, 108, 126, 144
Thompson, D. W., 189
Thompson, F. C., 4
Thompson, J. A., 54
Thompson, W. M., 12
Thompson, W. R., 23
Tillapaugh, F., 186
Timmons, H. E., 174
Torrey, R. A., 125, 165, 172
Tournier, R. E., 40, 84, 92
Towns, E. L., 185, 186, 193, 196
Trench, R. C., 68, 69, 70, 116
Turnbull, R. G., 147, 148, 163
Turner, G. A., 12
Tozer, A. W., 126, 136, 155, 171

U

Unger, M. F., 7, 11, 12, 19, 20, 62, 152

V

Vaughan, C. J., 85, 100
Vincent, M. C., 100

Vine, W. E., 53, 95, 105, 114, 127
Virkler, H. A., 10
Vos, H. F., 12, 208

W

Wagner, C. P., 186, 187
Wagner, D. M., 152
Wagner, G., 33
Wald, O., 169
Walker, F. D., 160
Waltke, B. K., 20
Walvoord, J. F., 56, 103, 116, 127, 140, 141, 142
Wardlaw, R., 49, 50
Warfield, B. B., 9, 127, 132
Wenham, G. J., 33
Westcott, B. F., 81, 98, 101, 108, 113, 138
West, N., 142
Wheat, E., 174
Whitcomb, J. C., Jr., 29, 34, 42, 56
White, R. E. O., 86
White, W., Jr., 20
Whitesell, F. D., 151, 152, 185
Whyte, A., 130, 158, 179
Wiersbe, W. W., 77, 139, 159, 161
Wight, F. H., 14
Wigram, G. W., 22, 66
Wiley, H. O., 123
Wilkerson, David, 190
Wilkerson, Don, 190
Wilson, W., 21
Wiseman, D. J., 24
Wiseman, L. H., 37
Wood, A. S., 89
Wood, L. J., 13, 39, 51